TIME : SPACE

Landscape Architecture in the Nation's Capital

ASLA Potomac Chapter

POTOMAC

ASLA

THE
DONNING COMPANY
PUBLISHERS

ME : SPACE

pe Architecture in the Nation's Capital

ASLA Potomac Chapter

Edited by
Adele N. Ashkar, ASLA
Bethany A. Carton, ASLA
Ron M. Kagawa, ASLA, LEED AP

TIME : SPACE

Landscape Architecture in the Nation's Capital

is dedicated to the
Potomac Chapter Membership,
who by their own participation will continue the legacy of
Landscape Architecture
in the National Capital area.

Contents

Introduction

On the occasion of the 2010 American Society of Landscape Architects Annual Meeting in Washington, DC, the TIME : SPACE Project presents the Potomac Chapter's three-year effort to record the voices of our membership and their contributions to the body of knowledge of landscape architecture in the National Capital area.

TIME : SPACE, Landscape Architecture in the Nation's Capital offers glimpses of the Chapter's evolution over its lifespan through a historical overview, facilitated public discussions with elders, contemporary professionals and students, and a sampling of contemporary works by the membership. As the first-ever published record of its kind, *TIME : SPACE* represents the Potomac Chapter's past, present and, through the vision of its students, the Chapter's shared future.

"I think the cell phone has had more of an impact on the practice of landscape architecture profession than the computer, because you can call into the office while out in the field," said retired Ohio State Professor Brooks Breeden in response to moderator Bill Thompson's queries about changes in the profession. Brooks was one of nine elders who participated in the Chapter's 2008 National Landscape Architecture Month public symposium at Brookside Gardens in Wheaton, Maryland.

"A recession is a terrible thing to waste!" argued a passionate Steve Lefton during the spirited discourse of the Chapter's 2009 National Landscape Architecture Month Contemporaries/ Principals Forum. Steve was one of thirty-one firm principals, corporate executive officers, executives, and agency chiefs representing the contemporary state of the profession in proceedings at the Jack Morton Auditorium on the Washington, DC campus of The George Washington University.

"I'm thinking less about how my peers would be thinking about me than about the people who've spent time within my spaces and enjoyed them, even if they didn't know it was my work!" said a reflective Evelyn Nolan, a recent graduate student of The George Washington University as she pondered moderator Lisa Siri's questions to students addressing how they would like their peers to remember them. Her comments were made during proceedings recorded at the University's Alexandria, Virginia campus in November 2009.

The TIME : SPACE Project has been made possible by the gracious and humbling support of Potomac Chapter's 2007, 2008, 2009, and 2010 Executive Committees, an American Society of Landscape Architects Chapter Improvement Grant, and pecuniary support by firms that provided assistance in the publication of their folio works.

The history of the Potomac Chapter reflects the history of the American Society of Landscape Architects (ASLA) as an organization, and the growth of landscape architecture as a profession in the United States. Responding to world wars, national emergencies, and national celebrations, the Potomac Chapter has provided a pool of talented, nationally recognized practitioners who have contributed enormously to America's public realm and private quality of life. In the last quarter of the twentieth century, this contribution has extended beyond the Chapter's local region to include the creation of significant works of landscape architecture all over the world. The landscapes of US Embassies worldwide, major new parks in Boston, Pennsylvania, Tennessee, and elsewhere represent the indelible mark of the Potomac Chapter's members at the national and international level, as well as locally. Chapter professionals also have been leaders in fostering development of international landscape architectural organizations. Although many landscape professionals from the nation and the world have worked within Washington, DC, and the region, Potomac Chapter members since the early 1900s have had a significant influence in forming the Federal City as we know it today.

The Washington, DC Chapter of ASLA: 1938 through 1950

In 1899, the American Society of Landscape Architects (ASLA) was formed by members from Massachusetts and New York. By 1919, following World War I, several professionals from the Washington, DC area were members of ASLA, including James Gilbert Langdon, Professor Tell William Nicolet of the US War Department, and Charles P. Punchard, Jr., also of the US War Department. By that time, only four chapters of ASLA were established nationally: New York, Boston, Minnesota, and Midwest. In subsequent years, local memberships in ASLA continued to grow.

During the 1930s, ASLA annual meeting notes indicate a diminished level of professional activity, especially in the central and southern parts of the country, resulting from the extraordinarily difficult economic conditions of that period. But by the late 1930s, despite the difficulties of the Great

Depression, and due at least in part to the park and recreation component of the Works Progress Administration, the number of ASLA chapters had grown to eleven nationwide. In step with this nationwide trend, the Washington, DC Chapter of the ASLA was formally established in 1938, and by the time of the 1940 annual ASLA meeting, membership had grown to fifty-one professionals, many of whom were in government employ.

World War II took its profound global toll and affected the landscape architectural profession and local chapter activities as it did the rest of the American experience at the time. Washington, DC Chapter events included such presentations as a February 1942 Training Conference in Aerial Bombardment Protection sponsored by the Federal Office of Civilian Defense, the US Office of Education, and New York University. The Chapter's Program Committee also arranged for a series of meetings at which "outside speakers [will] advise landscape architects of the impact of the war on the National Capital, including expansion of the Federal Government and rapid increase in population." Chapter meeting minutes and notes from this time period note that members could suspend their dues during their service in the war. Seven chapter members were overseas in the military. Several members, including Louis Croft, a prisoner of war in Manila, Philippines, were granted a suspension of dues during their military duties. Among those in service abroad were Lieutenant Edward B. Ballard, and M. Meade Palmer, both of whom later became Fellows of ASLA. Palmer later went on to design the Lyndon Baines Johnson Memorial Grove on the Potomac, the first presidential memorial that was essentially a landscape solution, and he was later awarded the National ASLA Medal for the project.

By 1942, Rose Greely, FASLA, was an active member of the Washington, DC ASLA chapter.

January 16, 1948

Mr. Thomas C. Jeffers, President
D. C. Chapter
American Society of Landscape Architects
7013 Interior Building
Washington, D. C.

My dear Mr. Jeffers:

On behalf of the National Capital Park and Planning Commission I request that you designate some one fully cognizant of the interests and program of your association and also an alternate, to attend a meeting at 4:30 P. M. on Wednesday, January 28, 1948, in Room A, U. S. Chamber of Commerce.

The purpose of the meeting is the formation of a Citizens Advisory Board on the Plan of the National Capital and its Environs, so that our Commission can be assisted by some well considered and fully informed expression of the over-all non-official citizens' views and interests in the Comprehensive Plan on which a report is now being prepared for publication. Such a Citizens Advisory Board or Council has been successfully organized in several other cities and is believed to be an essential step in guiding the development of the city or metropolitan region in the best interests of all its inhabitants.

A similar invitation is being sent to many other organized citizens' groups whose participation is believed desirable and whose direct interest is obvious. While it is hoped thus to secure representation of all the important interests involved and of all kinds of experience and various points of view, it is not expected that members of the Board will after appointment in any way obligate the associations they represent, but that they will vote as individual members of the Board. On the other hand, they will be expected to keep their own associations informed of what is before the Board.

Trusting that we may have your cooperation in the formation of such a Citizens Advisory Board, and that you will notify me by letter or my office by telephone (Republic 1820, extension 2101) of the names and addresses of your two appointees,

Sincerely yours,

U. S. Grant, 3rd
Major General, U.S.A., Ret.
Chairman

Appointed Zach.
alternate Jeffers.

31431

Ulysses S. Grant III, chair of the National Capital Park and Planning Commission, was an advocate for the profession of landscape architecture.

With the end of World War II and the return to a more normal life, the Potomac Chapter focused its energy on pressing environmental protection, land use, and professional development issues. Nationally, the profession of landscape architecture was growing rapidly, and Chapter members were emerging to craft the public realm and private places in the Washington, DC region. The Chapter was also beginning to be active in recognizing significant individual contributions to the profession.

General Ulysses S. Grant III was nominated by the Potomac Chapter as a "corresponding member" of ASLA in 1942. Grant had had an extraordinary record of accomplishments in his service to the US Army Engineering Corps. From 1926 to 1933, as director of the Office of Public Buildings and Public Parks of the National Capital, he oversaw construction of ten parks, including Meridian Hill and the Lincoln Memorial Grounds. Working with Frederick Law Olmsted, Jr., and other great American landscape architects and architects, his project responsibilities also included the US Supreme Court, the Library of Congress Annex, the expansion of the US Capitol Grounds, and many more. He oversaw the Comprehensive Plan for Parks and Open Space, adding over two thousand acres of park and open space to the National Capital area, and sponsored legislation to expand this system further into Maryland. Grant became chair of the National Capital Planning Commission in 1942 and was finally elected a "corresponding member" of ASLA in 1946.

In 1948, the Chapter adopted its Constitution and Bylaws. In 1949, ASLA held its fiftieth anniversary annual meeting in Washington, DC. For the event, the

Rose Greely Urges Women to Study Landscape Architecture

By Jane Loye
Written for The Christian Science Monitor

Washington

If the American Society of Landscape Architects began a drive to encourage more students to enter their profession, Rose Greely would be among the most enthusiastic recruiters of women.

One of the few women members of the ASLA to be elected fellow as a result of outstanding work in landscape architecture, Miss Greely is keenly aware,

Awards Granted

Written for The Christian Science Monitor

Chicago

Industrial Designers Institute awards—awards given by designers for top styling—this year went to four Chicago men "for noteworthy and fresh approach to a design . . ."

The products judged were home scales and a series of integrated furnishings for school use.

Winners, awarded IDI gold medals, were Dave Chapman for his and his associates' work on school equipment, and Franz Wagner, Richard S. Latham and Don De Fano for the "flight scales." Manufacturers of the products are the Brunswick-Balke-Collender Co. (school equipment) and Borg-Erickson Corp. (scales).

Awards by the four-year-old IDI, which may be given for design of any manufactured item, are selected by a national panel

she says, of the need for good, well-trained architects in domestic landscaping. Furthermore, "It is a tremendous field for women, and it's too bad more aren't going into it," the tall, gracious artist contends.

Last year, she recalls, Harvard University graduated only three women from its School of Design as landscape architects; two of them intended to work with their architect husbands. There were not enough women graduates to fill available positions.

While many men go into city planning, women have a great opportunity in domestic landscaping.

A prospective landscape architect, in Miss Greely's opinion, must draw well, with a sense of design and imagination, and should obtain either three years of specialized graduate work or four to five years of undergraduate study.

Favorite Subject

Rose Greely invariably directs conversation away from herself. She's delighted when it turns to her favorite subject, landscape architecture. While she talks about landscaping, her youthful face lightens with an irrepressible smile.

Her ultimate achievement has combined a love of art with a love of the outdoors, but before discovering the way to merge these two interests in one career, she did silversmithing in

terior decorating at the Art Institute of Chicago.

Following study at the Cambridge School for Domestic and Landscape Architecture, now part of Harvard University, she wrote for House and Garden and House Beautiful. Then she began her own architectural practice, transforming natural scenery from random growth of plants to beautiful arrangements of trees, shrubs, and flowers.

Since about 1925, she has con-

Fresh Fillip

Written for The Christian Science Monitor

For a new fillip to an old taste treat, here are two ideas:

To whipped cream add chocolate syrup to taste, after the cream is stiff. As a topping for plain custards and tapioca pudding the chocolate whipped cream will add an interesting new flavor.

For a little fancier sandwich filling, to cream cheese and nuts add bananas and cranberries. First run the nuts through the nut grinder, then grind whole fresh cranberries and regrind both together. Mix as you cream the banana and cheese together, adding a drop or two of milk to make a paste.

The filling is best when made fresh. One-third of a three-ounce package of cream cheese, about half a banana, and 10 to 20 each of nuts and cranberries, make several open-face sandwiches—enough to serve two.

tinued a private practice, and has at present, as her staff, an assistant landscape architect and part-time secretary. Her office is located in her charming Georgetown house which was the home of her father, the late Major General A. W. Greely, famous polar explorer and author.

Miss Greely enjoys variety in her work, designing the grounds for both small and large houses in town and country, for schools, and private institutions. "I never have the same request twice," she says.

A challenge is what she welcomes. "It is fun to do jobs that give you a problem right in the beginning," she says. Because she starts with an attempt to realize her client's viewpoint, her work cannot be classified as either formal or informal; it is flexible. She believes an architect should never try to force his ideas on a client; instead he must design what the client wants to live with.

Clients' Ideas

This native Washingtonian adapts her art to useful purpose. For the owner of a Washington inn, she planned a large cutting garden to supply flowers for decoration. For parents with young children, she moved fences of a play area to one side of the house where they would not cut off a view of the garden and dogwood trees.

To improve the appearance of a plain brick façade of the Leo Bernsteins' Washington house,

and white wisteria trained flat and high against the wall. An espalier vine, which displays red berries in the fall and white flowers in spring, adds color and interest.

Since the Bernsteins leave Washington during the summer, they wanted a garden that would look attractive all winter. Miss Greely's solution was to pave the center of the small square garden with flagstone, since the area was too small for both grass and terrace. In each of the four corners she placed a crape myrtle tree and primroses.

Local Materials

As a rule she likes to use materials typical of the surrounding countryside. To pave a terrace in Sea Island, Georgia, she used tabby with an aggregate of ground, colored shells in a pattern of alternating strips of tabby cyprus.

Recognition of Rose Greely's flair for achieving beautiful effects with shrubs and flowers came to her when ASLA appointed her to the first advisory committee to assist in restoring Williamsburg. Also the Washington Board of Trade has twice awarded her work.

"She has helped to make the field of landscape architecture a distinguished one here," said one of her Washington colleagues recently. As a pioneer in the Capital's landscaping, "she has made it landscape architecture instead of landscape gardening. She is a good designer and has led the way for

Rose Greely, FASLA, achieved media attention in this 1953 *Washington Star* article.

Chapter prepared a map of the local region, including 116 open spaces, parks, and places of significance. It was a proud moment for the eleven-year-old Washington, DC Chapter, since attendees included Frederick Law Olmsted, Jr., Norman Newton, Miss [sic] Rose Greely, Stanley Abbott, Charles Gillette, Conrad Wirth, and many other landscape luminaries of the period.

The Potomac Chapter: 1951 and Beyond

As the Chapter grew, collaboration with the Virginia and Maryland Chapters increased. In 1951, the name of the "Washington, DC Chapter" was officially changed to the "Potomac Chapter of the American Society of Landscape Architects." Since then, the Chapter has had a significant impact on

ROSE GREELY · LANDSCAPE ARCHITECT

8181 O STREET, WASHINGTON 7, D. C.

FELLOW, AMERICAN SOCIETY OF LANDSCAPE ARCHITECTS   REGISTERED ARCHITECT, DISTRICT OF COLUMBIA

May 25th 1956

Mr. Morris Trotter
President Washington Chapter, ASLA
Washington, D.C.

Dear Mr. Trotter:-

      I want to express my appreciation to you and to
the whole Chapter, for the delightful dinner that you gave in
my honor. I think you are starting a very nice precededent,
which you will have to live up to, when other members of the
Chapter retire. I can't tell you what a warm feeling it gives
to those who are on the way out.

      The orchids are still lovely and I am still
wearing them with pleasure. Many thanks to the Chapter again.
And I shall telephone Mr. Coplen to tell him what a nice thought
it was on his part, to give so many seedlings of Azalea Rose
Greely.

      I am hoping to be away next winter, although I
shall have to return in the late fall to rent my house again,
before I go. But I hope that if I am in Washington again in 1958
I shall be allowed to come to some of the Chapter meetings.

      Sincerely yours,

      Rose Greely

When Greely retired, in 1956, the Washington Chapter celebrated her career with a banquet in her honor.

ASLA as a national organization, with many Potomac Chapter members holding office in ASLA's national leadership and six members serving as National ASLA president since 1953. From the 1950s through the 1960s, the Potomac Chapter was at a high level of activity and influence. Although the nation was at war in Korea and later in Vietnam until the 1970s, the Chapter's records indicate little local effect of these events on local professional activities.

In support of federal legislation, such as the Open Space and Urban Development Act of 1961, the Highway Beautification Act of 1965 and the initiative to establish licensing for landscape architects in Virginia, Chapter activities and Chapter members continued to have a profound influence on the local region.

Also during this time, landscape architects of the Potomac Chapter continued to distinguish themselves nationally. Conrad Wirth, FASLA, became director of the National Park Service (NPS) in 1951, and in 1961 won a Rockefeller Public Service Award, among many other honors. Upon Wirth's retirement in 1964, the *Washington Star* newspaper dubbed him "Mr. Park Service." Stanley Abbott, FASLA, who had been principal designer of the Shenandoah National Forest Park, and the Skyline Drive, was recognized by the National Park Service with the naming of the park's Lake Abbott in his honor.

In the 1960s, during President Lyndon Baines Johnson's administration, First Lady 'Lady Bird' Johnson initiated her Beautification Program. Begun in the Nation's Capital, the program was later expanded nationwide. Numerous Potomac Chapter members were involved in this effort—as members of the Beautification Task Force established within the National Park Service's National Capital Parks, and in Washington, DC offices that participated in an interagency effort to coordinate beautification efforts throughout the city. Mrs. Johnson was later made an honorary member of ASLA for her efforts in support of environmental quality and design, and of landscape architecture as a profession. The Highway Beautification Act of 1965 and other environmental laws were direct results of these efforts. With Meade Palmer, FASLA, playing a key role, along with Raymond Freeman, FASLA; Ed Ballard, FASLA; and others, the Chapter was instrumental in naming "Olmsted Island" in the Potomac River. The island became a Memorial to John Charles Olmsted and Frederick Law Olmsted, Jr., and the role they played in the shaping of Washington, DC. This action was initiated by the Potomac Chapter and the island was dedicated on April 22, 1965.

During the 1970s, the Chapter once again updated and revised its Constitution and Bylaws, and continued its path of activism. Chapter member Raymond Freeman, FASLA, not only served as National ASLA president, but also served as deputy director of the National Park Service, received the ASLA President's Medal, and was director of ASLA Government Affairs after his retirement from the National Park Service. In 1975, a group of Chapter members began a detailed inventory of open spaces in Washington, DC. Later, this information was finalized and compiled by a Potomac Chapter Committee, working with James Matthew Evans, FASLA, as editor, in the book *The Landscape Architecture of Washington, D.C.: A Comprehensive Guide*, published in 1981. The Committee also wrote articles on the landscape architecture of Washington, DC, that

In October 1959, the *American Observer* featured landscape architecture as a promising career that is "almost always pleasant, creative, and challenging."

Conrad L. Wirth, Director of the National Park Service since 1951, entered Federal service in 1928 with the National Capital Park and Planning Commission after being graduated from Massachusetts Agriculture College. He entered NPS in 1931 as Assistant Director in charge of Land Planning. Wirth, 61, comes from a family dedicated to park service. His father was Superintendent of Parks in Minneapolis for 26 years, and one brother was Superintendent of Parks in New Haven. He and his wife, Helen, live at 3808 Leland st., Chevy Chase. They have two sons, Theodore and Peter.

Conrad Wirth, FASLA, was awarded a Rockefeller Public Service Award in 1961.

were printed as a special section of the November 1981 *Landscape Architecture Magazine* in conjunction with the 1981 ASLA annual meeting held that year in Washington, DC. Others who shaped the public realm included Lester Collins and Lawrence and Beatrice Coffin.

In 1976, Darwina Neal, FASLA, led the local Chapter effort, with support from ASLA National, to defeat a proposal by Harvard University to build a library expansion requiring removal and "reconstruction" of a portion of the historic gardens at Dumbarton Oaks in Washington, DC, originally designed by Beatrix Jones Farrand. A year of correspondence and meetings resulted in a major victory for ASLA and the Chapter, when Harvard agreed not to build the library under the gardens. Many years later the Dunbarton Oaks Research Library and Collection was built on another site, without disturbing the historic gardens.

In 1972 the Maryland Chapter was formed as an independent entity, followed by the establishment of the Virginia Chapter in 1978. The Potomac Chapter has continued to work collaboratively with its colleagues in both organizations: with Maryland, on a shared annual awards and banquet program, and with Virginia, on licensure for landscape architects. As a result of the collaboration with the Virginia Chapter, certification of landscape architects was signed into law in 1980 in the Commonwealth of Virginia.

The 1980s saw an economic boom that lasted until the end of that decade, and the contributions of the Potomac Chapter and its members continued to be extraordinary. Many Chapter individuals and firms created institutional, public, and residential landscapes that shaped the region. John Parsons, FASLA, ASLA National La Gasse Medal winner, represented the National Park Service on the National Capital Planning Commission for more than ten years. The Frederick Law Olmsted Papers Project had been started in 1973 by Charles Capen McLaughlin, Honorary ASLA, Potomac

Chapter. The first volume of the Olmsted Papers, published in 1977, began to make available a complete understanding of the thoughts and writings of America's first landscape architect. Eight volumes of the twelve-volume series have been published and the project continues today under the direction of Charles E. Beveridge, Honorary ASLA, Potomac Chapter, and ASLA National Olmsted Medal winner.

Projects designed by Oehme, van Sweden and Associates partners Wolfgang Oheme, FASLA, and James van Sweden, FASLA, and documented in their books, created a revolution in landscape design style called the "New American Garden" that has influenced the design of landscapes worldwide. The California firm of EDAW, founded by Garret Eckbo, Francis Dean, Don Austin, and Edward Williams, had established a fledgling office in Alexandria, Virginia, in 1975 to serve the needs of the burgeoning Washington metropolitan region. Under the leadership of Principal-in-Charge Joseph E. Brown, FASLA, National ASLA Medal winner, the firm grew explosively into the early 1980s. Brown brilliantly gathered a group of highly promising young professionals who helped propel the office forward and, within less than five years, established EDAW as a leader in the region. Between 1984 and 1988, seven of these young landscape architects established their own offices in the region, all leading nationally known, award-winning firms in their own right, all becoming Fellows of ASLA, and most becoming active members or officers of the Chapter. These firms continue to flourish today, and all remain supportive and engaged in Potomac Chapter activities.

Rockefeller Public Service Awards Of $3500 Won by Six Career Men

Six career civil servants, all area residents, were named yesterday by Robert F. Goheen, President of Princeton University, as recipients of the Rockefeller Public Service Awards for 1960-61.

The recipients were cited for "achievement and long and distinguished career service" in five areas of endeavor.

Each winner will receive a cash award of $3500. Moreover, he may draw additional funds, if he so desires, to make available his knowledge by devoting time to lecturing, writing, or pursuing a research program at the university of his choice, or by engaging in some other educational endeavor.

The winners are Robert M. Ball, Deputy Director of the Bureau of Old Age and Sur-

vivors Insurance, in the area of administration-general; Charles E. (Chip) Bohlen, Special Assistant to the Secretary of State (foreign affairs); Sterling B. Hendricks, Chief Scientist of the Mineral Nutrition Laboratory for Pioneering Research (science and technology).

Also, Richard E. McArdle, Chief of the Forest Service

Pictures on Page A8.

(conservation and resources); Leonard Niederlehner, Deputy General Counsel in the Office of the Secretary of Defense (law and regulation); Conrad L. Wirth, Director of National Park Service (conservation and resources).

The awards, made possible by a fund established in 1951

by John D. Rockefeller 3d, changed their complexion this year. In previous years, the awards were intended to make additional self-training possible for government employes in mid-career.

With the passage of the Training Act of 1958, which gave broad training authority to all executive agencies of the Government, a principal objective of the original awards was realized.

The project is administered by Princeton's Woodrow Wilson School of Public and International Affairs. The selections were recommended by a committee, composed of distinguished Americans with a wide knowledge of government affairs, but not connected with the Federal Government or Princeton.

The Rockefeller Award honored Wirth, director of the National Park Service, in the category of "conservation and resources."

The past two decades have continued with success for the Potomac Chapter. Following its Strategic Plan, adopted in 1995, and updated in 2002, the Chapter continues to provide activities, conferences, social gatherings, and lectures for established professionals and emerging professionals alike. With membership currently over three hundred, the Potomac Chapter has continued to support Virginia licensing efforts. In 2009, regulations were upgraded, making landscape architecture a licensed, instead of certified, profession in the Commonwealth of Virginia. Chapter members continue to excel. The Cultural Landscape Foundation, established by Charles Birnbaum, FASLA, National La Gasse and ASLA President's Medal winner, has grown to be a national force in raising awareness about the cultural value of historic landscapes and the recognition of landscape architecture as an art form. Sarah Boasberg, Honorary ASLA, was instrumental in the establishment of the Casey Trees Foundation, a leading activist group in the greening of Washington, DC. In his role as landscape architect overseeing US Embassy landscape design for the US Department of State, Alain DeVergie, FASLA, has created a culture within that organization that integrates landscape architecture as a crucial component of all new US Embassies worldwide. This effort has led to participation by many landscape architecture firms, both within the region and nationally, in projects all over the world. In addition to all of these accomplishments, Potomac Chapter members have authored nationally recognized books on landscape history, landscape design, horticulture and planning, and have developed methods of sustainable design that have become standard professional practice today.

Over its seventy-two years of history, the Potomac Chapter has nominated many honorary ASLA members and winners of the La Gasse, Olmsted, and other national professional medals. From presidents' wives to senators, congressional representatives and mayors, from high-ranking civil servants to nationally known scholars, the Chapter has seen its candidates elected to the highest honors ASLA can bestow. The Potomac Chapter has made a significant mark on the design of the public realm. Our members have shaped the Federal City, fostered coherent and environmentally sound legislation, promoted and protected the historic legacy of designed landscapes throughout America, and been national leaders in the practice of sustainable, regenerative design.

Today, as the members of the Potomac Chapter of the American Society of Landscape Architects consider our time and space, we are proud of this history, and we will foster the Chapter's legacy with energy and enthusiasm.

Faye Harwell, FASLA
September 2010

Acknowledgments, History chapter:

Martin Luther King Library,
Washingtoniana Collection, Washington, DC:
Derek Gray

ASLA National Headquarters:
Susan Cahill-Aylward, Honorary ASLA
Brook Hinrichs
Mary Hanson, Honorary ASLA

Individuals:
Charles Beveridge, Honorary ASLA, Olmsted
  Medal Winnner
Emily Chisholm
Ravi Desai
Margaret Herndon
Heather Hammatt Modzelewski, ASLA
Grace Lockwood, archive donor
Darwina Neal, FASLA
Deana Rhodeside
Elliot Rhodeside, FASLA

of the Potomac Chapter of ASLA

1899 American Society of Landscape Architects founded.

1916 American Society of Landscape Architects, Inc., becomes a chartered corporation in Massachusetts. There are four national chapters: New York, Boston, Minnesota, and Midwest.

1918 Four ASLA members are listed in the Washington, DC area: Theodora Kimball, James Gilbert Langdon, Tell William Nicolet, and Charles P. Punchard, Jr.

1919 ASLA has 102 members nationwide, including 50 Fellows.

1920s ASLA president A. D. Taylor leads a committee on "Professional Ethics and Practice Relative to Specific Charges and Methods of Charging" for landscape architects. Local members participate. In 1923, the report is submitted to national members.

1926– Major Ulysses S. Grant III is director of Public Buildings
1933 and Public Parks of the National Capital. He leads overseas landscape architects from all over the country and construction of ten parks, including Meridian Hill, Lincoln Memorial Grounds, and much of Rock Creek Parkway.

1935 ASLA Annual Report cites diminished national activity especially in the central and southern parts of the country.

1937 ASLA has six chapters: New York, Boston, Ohio-Michigan, Mississippi Valley, Pacific Coast, and Southeastern.

1938 ASLA has eleven chapters and its roster includes eighteen Members and three Junior Associates from the Washington, DC area, including Chevy Chase, Maryland, and Arlington, Virginia. Rose Greely and Charles W. Elliot II are among them. At the 1938 ASLA annual meeting, the trustees recommend that more local chapters be established in order to better serve the membership.

1938   The Washington, DC Chapter of the ASLA is officially established. There is no chapter activity noted in ASLA National reports until 1940.

1942   The Washington, DC Chapter notifies members of a "Training Conference in Aerial Bombardment Protection" sponsored by the Federal Office of Civilian Defense, US Office of Education, and New York University. The chapter Program Committee arranges a series of meetings in which "outside speakers advise landscape architects on the impact of the war on the National Capital including expansion of the Federal Government, and a rapid increase in population."

A report is prepared by the Washington, DC Chapter: "Camouflage—Here and Now" describing methods of site planning for camouflage from the air.

Sir Jeffrey Jellicoe visits Washington to meet with Chapter officers about encouraging young people to enter the building and landscape trades. The Chapter nominates Jellicoe as ASLA "corresponding member."

Chapter members listed in the meeting minutes as overseas include: Lieutenant Edward Ballard; Leonard Bartlett, Jr.; Chester W. Nichols; Meade Palmer; Maurice Plotkin; and Louis Croft (in internment camp).

1943   *Remember Us in 1943* is published by the Chapter. It is a public communication to seek support for the profession of landscape architecture during the war years when work was greatly diminished.

1946   Major General Ulysses S. Grant III is elected as corresponding member of ASLA Washington, DC Chapter. At the time of his election, Grant is chair of the National Capital Planning Commission.

1948   The Washington, DC Chapter adopts its Bylaws. Included in its territory are Virginia, Maryland, and the District of Columbia.

1949   ASLA holds its fiftieth anniversary annual meeting in Washington, DC. A map of the region prepared by the Chapter is provided to attendees, noting 116 open spaces and places of interest and national significance. Outstanding members attending the meeting include Major General Ulysses S. Grant III; Rose Greely, FASLA; Charles Gillette, FASLA; Stanley Abbott, FASLA; and Conrad Wirth. Attendees also include Norman Newton, and Mr. and Mrs. Frederick Law Olmsted, Jr.

1951   The Chapter changes its name from the Washington, DC Chapter to the Potomac Chapter. Chapter member Conrad L. Wirth, FASLA, becomes director of the US Department of Interior, National Park Service.

1953   The *Evening Star* newspaper runs an article crediting the Potomac Chapter for bringing concern about the condition of the National Mall to the attention of President Dwight D. Eisenhower.

1960   A Potomac Chapter committee proposes the designation of an Olmsted memorial within Washington, DC. Meade Palmer, FASLA, leads the effort.

1961   The Chapter adopts its Constitution and Bylaws. The Open Space and Urban Development Act of 1961 is proposed to establish the value of open space and parks in urban areas. The Potomac Chapter's statement of support, drafted by members including Norman Newton, FASLA, is read at US Senate Hearing S858 on February 9.

1962   The Chapter works closely with Virginia members to initiate the establishment of professional licensing for landscape architects in Virginia.

1963   A chapter Committee on Registration is formed. Despite all efforts, Virginia House Bill No. 478 fails to pass.

1964   Conrad Wirth, FASLA, retires from the National Park Service.

1965   Olmsted Island is dedicated. Baltimore's Peale Museum hosts an exhibit of original drawings of works by the Olmsted firm, organized with the help of the Potomac

Chapter. Chapter members speak at hearings in support of the Highway Beautification Act of 1965.

1972   Constitution and Bylaws of the Potomac Chapter are revised. The official name of the chapter becomes the Potomac Chapter of the American Society of Landscape Architects, Inc.

1975   The Chapter begins an inventory of open spaces and parks in Washington, DC. By 1976, the inventory is largely completed and includes places of interest within the city and the nearby region. Eventually, the inventory becomes the basis for the 1981 book *The Landscape Architecture of Washington, D.C.: A Comprehensive Guide* by James Matthew Evans, FASLA.

1976   The Potomac Chapter works with ASLA National to defeat a proposal to reconstruct a portion of Dumbarton Oaks. Darwina Neal, FASLA, leads the effort to protect the gardens by Beatrix Farrand, FASLA.

1978   The Virginia Chapter of the ASLA is formed as an independent chapter. Virginia and Potomac continue to work closely on many issues, particularly state licensing for landscape architects.

1980   Governor John Dalton signs the bill designating landscape architecture as a "Certified" profession in

1982 ASLA holds its annual meeting in Washington, DC. The Chapter commissions a commemorative silkscreen artwork for the occasion. Betty Kubalak, regionally and nationally recognized artist, produces a limited edition of 250 of this work.

1983 Chapter secretary Grace Lockwood donates her collection of Chapter records to the Washingtoniana Collection of the Martin Luther King, Jr. Library in Washington, DC. The archive is available to the public and is maintained for the Chapter by the library archivists in perpetuity.

1983– The Chapter's membership grows to over three hundred.
1988 At least seven new, significant landscape architecture firms are established in the region following the economic prosperity in the region and the nation.

1992 ASLA holds its annual meeting in Washington, DC.

1994 Author David Grayson Allen conducts interviews for his book *The Olmsted National Historic Site and the Growth of Historic Landscape Preservation*. Potomac Chapter members interviewed include Raymond L. Freeman, FASLA.

1995 The Chapter initiates a Strategic Plan to chart its activities for the future. Focus groups are held during the year and attended by members, Fellows, and honorary members. The plan is adopted in spring 1995.

2001 Edward Ballard Scholarship is established by the Chapter to support students with their professional training tuition.

2006 The Chapter's program for National Landscape Architecture Month, "The Confluence of Water and Design on the Mall," a tour of four featured designs along the National Mall, wins a community outreach award from ASLA National. The first Virginia Licensure Summit is held jointly by the Virginia and Potomac Chapters. In support of ASLA National's "50 by 2010" program to obtain state licensing on a nationwide basis, the goal is to obtain regulatory upgrade from certification to licensure.

2007 The Time : Space Project is conceived. The project is designed to document the history of the Potomac Chapter, understand its past and current contributions to the region's landscape and professional activities, and chart opportunities for emerging professionals. ASLA National awards a Chapter Initiative Program (CIP) grant to aid in supporting the effort.

2009 The Commonwealth of Virginia approves state licensing for Virginia landscape architects, upgrading the profession's regulatory status from certification to licensure!

2010 *Time : Space, Landscape Architecture in the Nation's Capital* is published on the occasion of the 2010 ASLA annual meeting, held in Washington, DC.

Bibliography

Martin Luther King Jr. Memorial Library, Washington, DC
Washingtoniana Collection: Potomac Chapter of the American
Society of Landscape Architects

1941–1945

Box 4: Training Conference in Aerial Bombardment Program.

Box 4: Wehrly, Max S. "Letter." 28 May 1942.

Box 4: Williams, Bradford. "Letter." 29 June 1942.

Box 4: Williams, Bradford. "Letter." 11 July 1942.

Box 6: Hornbeck, Henry L. *Camouflage—Here and Now*. 17 August 1942.

Box 6: *American Society of Landscape Architects: Washington Chapter Meeting*. 28 October 1942: 1–2.

Box 4: Williams, Bradford. "Letter." 27 November 1942.

Box 6: *American Society of Landscape Architects: Washington Chapter Executive Committee Meeting*. 3 November 1942.

Box 6: *American Society of Landscape Architects: Washington Chapter Executive Committee Meeting*. December 1942.

Box 6: Turrell, Cornelia, H. "Letter." 11 October 1943.

Box 6: *American Society of Landscape Architects Publications Board*. 1943.

Box 4: *American Society of Landscape Architects: Washington Chapter*.

1946–1950

Box 6: Ballard, Edward B. "Letter." 19 February 1948.

Box 6: Jeffers, Thomas C. "Letter." 19 February 1946.

Box 6: Zach, Leon. "Letter." 9 December 1946.

Box 6: Jeffers, Thomas C. *Ulysses S. Grant, 3rd Major General, Corps of Engineers, U.S. Army*: 1–4.

Box 6: Grant, U. S. "Letter." 16 January 1948.

Box 6: Hubbard, Henry. "Letter." 18 August 1947.

Box 6: American Society of Landscape Architects: Washington Chapter. *Summary of Constitution and Bylaws*. December 1948.

Box 6: American Society of Landscape Architects. *ASLA Bulletin: Fiftieth Anniversary Meeting*. February 1949.

Box 6: *American Society of Landscape Architects, 50th Anniversary Field Trips*. 1949.

Box 6: Jeffers, Thomas C. "Letter." 19 April 1949.

Box 6: American Society of Landscape Architects: Washington Chapter. *Minutes of the December 11, 1950 Meeting*. 14 December 1950.

Box 9: American Society of Landscape Architects: Washington Chapter. *Suggested Program for 1949–1950*. 1949.

1951–1960

Box 7: American Society of Landscape Architects. *ASLA Bulletin*, January 1951: 167.

Box 7/8: American Society of Landscape Architects: Washington Chapter. "Letter." 25 February 1951.

Box 7/8: American Society of Landscape Architects: Potomac Chapter. "Letter." 2 March 1951.

Box 6: American Society of Landscape Architects: Potomac Chapter. *The Executive Committee's Annual Report to the Board of Trustees for the Year 1951.* 1951.

Box 3: American Society of Landscape Architects: Potomac Chapter Public Relations Committee. *Public Relations Idea for the American Society of Landscape Architects.* 10 December 1951.

Box 6: American Society of Landscape Architects: Potomac Chapter. *The President's and Secretary-Treasurer's Annual Report for the Year 1953.* 1953.

Box 3: Leye, Jane. "Rose Greely Urges Women to Study Landscape Architecture." *Washington Star,* 1953.

Box 3: American Society of Landscape Architects: Potomac Chapter. "Architects Ask Removal of Temporary Buildings." The *Evening Star,* 15 January 1953.

Box 3: McKelway, B. M, ed. "Time for a Change on the Mall." The *Evening Star,* 17 January 1953.

Box 3: Eckbo, Garrett. "Letter." 10 September 1953.

Box 7: American Society of Landscape Architects. *ASLA Bulletin,* June 1954: 407.

Box 7/8: American Society of Landscape Architects: Potomac Chapter. "Letter." 5 September 1954.

Box 2: American Society of Landscape Architects: Potomac Chapter. "Letter." 21 October 1954.

Box 9: American Society of Landscape Architects: Potomac Chapter. "Letter." 18 February 1955.

Box 2: American Society of Landscape Architects: Potomac Chapter. "List of Fellows, Members, and Associates." January 1956.

Box 2: Greely, Rose. "Letter." 25 May 1956.

Box 2: American Society of Landscape Architects. "Memo." 7 August 1956.

Box 2: United States Information Agency, State Department. "Memo." 1957.

Box 7/8: American Society of Landscape Architects: Washington, DC Chapter. "Letter." 27 December 1958.

Box 9: Berle, Anton. "Careers for Tomorrow As a Landscape Architect." *American Observer,* 12 October 1959.

Box 3: American Society of Landscape Architects: Potomac Chapter. *Report of the Olmsted Memorial Committee of the Potomac Chapter, ASLA.* Circa 1961.

Box 2: American Society of Landscape Architects: Potomac Chapter. "Report." Circa 1961.

1961–1970

Box 3: Palmer, Meade. *Report of the Olmsted Memorial Committee of the Potomac Chapter, ASLA.*

Box 3: Zion, Robert. "Letter." 5 June 1961.

Box 3: Schneck, Ray M. "Letter." 6 December 1961.

Box 3: Palmer, Meade. "Letter." 19 April 1962: 1–2.

Box 3: Fay, Fredrick A. "Letter." 21 May 1962.

Box 4: Clay, Grady. "Letter." 21 May 1963.

Box 9: Zach, Leon. "Statement in support of The Open Space and Urban Development Act of 1961," read at US Senate hearing S 858.

Box 4: Clay, Grady. "Letter." 28 May 1963.

Box 6: American Society of Landscape Architects: Potomac Chapter. *Newsletter*, January 1964.

Box 3: Freeman, Raymond L. "Letter." 3 March 1964.

Box 3: Olmsted Exhibition Committee. "Letter." 20 November 1964.

Box 4: 89th Congress of the United States of America, Public Law Act 89-285.

Box 2: United States Department of the Interior. National Park Service Brochure. *Prince William Forest Park*.

Box 2: American Society of Landscape Architects: Potomac Chapter. "Olmsted Memorial Invitation." 10 April 1965.

Box 2: The Peale Museum. "Letter." 8 March 1965.

Box 3: American Society of Landscape Architects. "Notice of Dedication of Olmsted Island." 14 April 1965.

Box 3: "News Release: Olmsted Exhibition." June 1964: 1–2.

Box 5: Office of the White House Press Secretary. "Press release in name of President Lyndon Baines Johnson." 26 May 1965.

Box 4: "House Joint Resolution: Directing the Virginia Advisory Legislative Council to make a study and report upon matters relating to the registration of landscape architects." 14 February 1966.

Box 3: American Society of Landscape Architects: Potomac Chapter. "Letter." 5 June 1966.

Box 3: American Society of Landscape Architects: Potomac Chapter. "Letter." 27 June 1966.

Box 3: American Society of Landscape Architects: Potomac Chapter. "Letter." 14 September 1966.

Box 5: American Society of Landscape Architects. "Memo to ASLA Chapter Presidents and Trustees." 18 March 1966.

Box 5: American Society of Landscape Architects: Potomac Chapter. "Letter." 6 March 1966.

Box 5: American Society of Landscape Architects. "Letter." 27 September 1965.

Box 5: American Society of Landscape Architects. "Career Guidance Awards Rules and Regulations." 15 November 1965.

Box 3: *Employment of Landscape Architects in the Federal Government*. 1970.

Box 5: *American Society of Landscape Architects*. 7 February 1965.

Box 5: American Society of Landscape Architects. *Resolution Regarding a National Program of Scenic Roads and Highways*. 13 February 1965.

Box 4: American Society of Landscape Architects: Potomac Chapter. "Letter." 28 March 1966: 1–5.

Box 2: American Society of Landscape Architects, Potomac Chapter. "Symposium on Landscape Architecture Education." February 1966.

Box 9: American Society of Landscape Architects Potomac Chapter. "Monthly Meeting." February 1970.

Box 9: News article (unidentified publication). "Federal Officials Receive Rockefeller Public Service Awards."

Box 9: American Society of Landscape Architects: Potomac Chapter. "Roster." January 1969.

Box 9: Palmer, Meade. "Letter." 29 November 1966.

Boxes 10, 11, 12: American Society of Landscape Architects: Potomac Chapter. "Notes from Potomac Chapter Archives: 1975–1976." 2009.

Box 9: Dodge, Carlton. "Mailgram." 15 February 1976.

Box 9: American Society of Landscape Architects: Potomac Chapter. *Constitution and Bylaws.* 6 December 1972: 1–17.

Box 9: American Society of Landscape Architects. "Memorandum." 27 January 1975.

1971–1980

Box 4: United States Department of the Interior, National Park Service. "Letter." Circa 1976.

Box 4: American Society of Landscape Architects: Potomac Chapter. "Letter." 12 May 1976.

Box 4: American Society of Landscape Architects: Potomac Chapter. "Letter." 23 February 1976.

Box 4: American Society of Landscape Architects: Potomac Chapter. "Letter." 20 February 1976.

Box 10: American Society of Landscape Architects: Potomac Chapter. "Guidebook Index." 23 February 1976.

Box 9: American Society of Landscape Architects Virginia Newsletter. "Dalton Signs Bill for Certification of L.A.'s in Virginia." 1980.

Box 9: "House Bill No. 805." 11 February 1974.

1991–2000

American Society of Landscape Architects: Potomac Chapter. *Strategic Plan for Potomac Chapter of ASLA.* Spring 1995.

2001–2009

New collection, unboxed. "Virginia Licensure Summit, Working List of Invited Participants." 6 July 2006.

New collection, unboxed. American Society of Landscape Architects: Potomac Chapter. "Notes from Potomac Chapter Archives: 1995–2006."

A=COM

"... **creating exemplary environments**." Since its original inception as the EDAW office in Alexandria in 1975, AECOM Design + Planning has contributed to the civic and private development of Washington, the region, and further afield, serving a wide variety of clients on projects of distinction and value to community, environment, and economy. A collaborative studio approach integrating environmental and urban planning with urban design and landscape architecture continues to spark creative thinking and innovative and client-responsive outcomes. Project types encompass city and regional plans, mixed-use and community design, military bases and communities, civic and public realm, historic and cultural sites, health and education immersive and campus environments, and sustainability, energy and environmental impact studies. A representative cross-section of the office's legacy and contemporary work is illustrated on the following pages.

Big Darby Water Resources Accord, Franklin County, Ohio, 2007
ASLA Merit Award/Chapter, 2007 First Place Award Ohio Planning Conference/Chapter

Washington Harbour, Washington, DC, 1988 Grand Award, NAIOP/Chapter

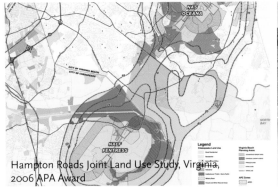

Hampton Roads Joint Land Use Study, Virginia, 2006 APA Award

Disney's Celebration Public Realm, Celebration, Florida, 2003 ASLA Merit Award/Chapters

Tidal Schuylkill River Master Plan,
Philadelphia, Pennsylvania,
2003 ASLA Merit Award/Planning Category/National

Orientation, Museum and Education Center at
Mount Vernon, Virginia, 2008 ASLA Honor Award/Chapter

Memorial to the 56 Signers of the Declaration of
Independence, Washington, DC,
1984 ASLA Honor Award/National

National Museum of the American Indian,
Washington, DC,
2006 ASLA Traveling Award (Highest Award)/Chapter

Wharf District Parks, Boston, Massachusetts,
2008 ASLA Honor Award/Chapter

Women in Military Service for America Memorial,
1998 ASLA Innovative Excellence Award (Highest Award),
1998 ASLA Honor Award/Chapter

Children's Garden Norfolk Botanical Garden,
Norfolk, Virginia,
2008 ASLA Honor Award/Chapter

Jefferson Expansion Memorial General
Management Plan and EIS, Saint Louis, Misouri

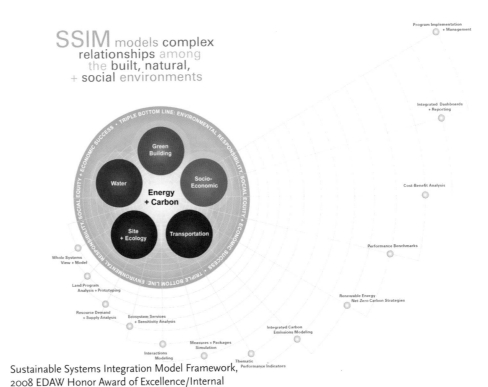

SSIM models complex
relationships among
the built, natural,
+ social environments

TRIPLE BOTTOM LINE: ENVIRONMENTAL RESPONSIBILITY, SOCIAL EQUITY + ECONOMIC SUCCESS • TRIPLE BOTTOM LINE: ENVIRONMENTAL RESPONSIBILITY, SOCIAL EQUITY + ECONOMIC SUCCESS • ECONOMIC SUCCESS

Green
Building

Water

Socio-
Economic

**Energy
+ Carbon**

Site
+ Ecology

Transportation

Program Implementation
+ Management

Integrated Dashboards
+ Reporting

Cost-Benefit Analysis

Performance Benchmarks

Renewable Energy
Net-Zero Carbon Strategies

Integrated Carbon
Emissions Modeling

Thematic
Performance Indicators

Measures + Packages
Simulation

Interactions
Modeling

Ecosystem Services
+ Sensitivity Analysis

Resource Demand
+ Supply Analysis

Land Program
Analysis + Prototyping

Whole Systems
View + Model

Sustainable Systems Integration Model Framework,
2008 EDAW Honor Award of Excellence/Internal

Navy Yard Master Plan, Washington, DC

American University Campus Master Plan and
Landscape Design, Washington, DC

Woodland Park, Herndon, Virginia
2007 ASLA Honor Award/Chapter

AECOM Design + Planning is a global land resource-based design and planning practice, part of the national and international multidisciplinary firm AECOM, with offices across the country and around the world. Our holistic approach to place-making creates communities, environments, and buildings that reduce carbon emissions, conserve natural resources, promote biodiversity, generate economic development, and improve social conditions. We are interested in significant work measured not by size, but by relevance to stakeholders, community, and setting.

Signature projects around the world include master plan and implementation design for the 2012 Olympics in London, the World Trade Center public realm design in New York City, urban design of the Tokyo Midtown, and master plan/lead consultant of Saadiyat Island Cultural District in Abu Dhabi. Current work includes: Baku Urban Parks (Azerbaijan), New Delhi Embassy (India), Pearl Harbor Cultural Landscape Report (Hawaii), Capital Space Plan (DC), Children's Garden at the Penn State Arboretum (Pennsylvania), National Museum of the U.S. Army (Virginia), Eilan Town Center (Texas), Anacostia/Bolling Master Plan (DC), Neighborhood Sustainability Indicators Pilot Project (DC), Prince George's County-Wide Water Resource Plan (Maryland), Potomac Yard Park (Virginia), GW Mount Vernon Campus Master Plan, NCPC Monumental Core Framework Plan (DC), EIS for the National Museum of African American Heritage and Culture (DC), and the National Eisenhower Memorial (DC).

Muhammad Ali Plaza, Louisville, Kentucky

Engineering Quadrangle, Cornell University, Ithaca, New York

National Capital Framework Plan, Washington, DC, 2008 ASLA Honor Award/Chapter

US Patent and Trademark Office Headquarters, Alexandria, Virginia, 2007 ASLA Merit Award/Chapter

Naval Station Rota Master Plan, Spain, 2005 APA Outstanding Federal Planning Project Award

Discovery Headquarters, Bethesda, Maryland, 2006 ASLA Merit Award/Chapter

Kimley-Horn combines national experience with a local sensibility for our clients in urban design, town planning, and landscape architecture. Renowned for our work on redevelopment, streetscape, and urban revitalization, our landscape architects and planners emphasize a pragmatic approach to sustainable design.

Kimley-Horn
and Associates, Inc.

On April 25, 2008, the Potomac Chapter launched its Time : Space Project with a day of round-table conversations at Brookside Gardens in Wheaton, Maryland. The first of three events, the symposium featured the Potomac Chapter's senior members in a meaningful celebration of National Landscape Architecture Month. Many of our elder members have enjoyed long, effective, and influential careers, and this event focused on the depth of knowledge, wisdom, and experience that they have accumulated. The following are highly abridged excerpts from the discussions of the day.

Session One: The Evolution of Your Career

Moderator: Lisa E. Delplace, ASLA

Participants: Kathryn S. Cochrane, ASLA; Robert H. Mortensen, FASLA; and Darwina L. Neal, FASLA

Edited by Adele N. Ashkar, ASLA

Kathryn Cochrane

In 1957 Kathryn Cochrane graduated from Penn State University with a degree in landscape architecture. After working in private practice, she became the first female landscape architect hired by the Eastern Division of the National Park Service. As a public practitioner she designed campgrounds, planting plans, roads and interpretive developments for battlefields, and sometimes supervised implementation of the work. She came to Washington, DC, to work in Lady Bird Johnson's Beautification Program. In addition, she designed several small parks built in the Capital City. Always an artist, she has increasingly devoted herself to watercolor painting since the 1970s. A longtime member of the Springfield Art Guild and the Potomac Valley Water Colorists, she has exhibited her work regularly throughout the Washington, DC, area.

Voices of Our Elders

"I worked at the National Park Service, and my work designing one of the Washington parks was discussed in a 1967 *National Geographic* article. In July 2007, when Lady Bird [Johnson] died, there was a picture in the paper [of me] with Lady Bird when she was working on her planting."

—Kathryn Cochrane

Moderator: "How did you become interested in landscape architecture?"

Cochrane: "As a girl, from a very young age I started gardening, doing all kinds of things, including being responsible, by the time I was twelve years old, for the design of our property at home. It just evolved that landscape architecture would be a way that I could continue this work. I moved back here in 1969 with my husband Doug and started landscape architecture work on our own property: I designed it to limit water run-off, used gravel to prevent water run-off . . . I designed it to preserve trees and native species. I also rescued plants from planned development areas . . . and today we still have some mountain laurel as result of that effort. Yes we do have invasives. As you recall forty years ago we were not aware of the whole mess related to invasive species.

Kathryn Cochrane describes her role outside the National Park Service as an "unpaid landscape architect activist and supervisor." Since the 1970s, she has intervened successfully in many public works projects that affected the quality of life in residential neighborhoods. She saved trees by convincing Fairfax County to narrow the right-of-way of a neighborhood sewer project from fifty feet to forty feet, carefully watching over the three-year project to prevent further damage to the landscape. Sixteen years later, the last site-supervisor on that project commented to her that she would never know how much she had taught others on that job: "A lot of things had been changed in Fairfax County as a result of my work," Kathryn observed. Calling herself an environmental landscape consultant, in the 1990s, Kathryn designed and started a "Creation Awareness Center" at a church. She laid out a trail on the grounds with both ecological and theological stops, calling it "The Living Cathedral." Kathryn taught eco-theological care and stewardship, using her paintings to illustrate concepts of environmental awareness. She relates a telling story from that time:

Cochrane: "One summer there was a Bible School in which two churches cooperated. I was teaching in the Creation Center and gave some Junior High kids some pencils and a sketchpad. I asked them to go out on the trail and 'sketch what you see. Don't worry about making art, just sketch.' The next year a mother came back, . . . whose son had been out on the trail the year before sketching [and she told me], 'You changed his life; now he sketches everywhere.'"

In addition to her painting, Kathryn still intervenes in area projects today: In 2000, she challenged Mt. Vernon's approach to planning parking areas for their new development. In 2008, she and her neighbors were still meeting with NPS and FHWA to find solutions to the parking issue.

Bob Mortensen

An ASLA Fellow, Bob Mortensen received his MLA from the University of Michigan in 1965, and a BS in landscape architecture from Ohio State University. He has worked in private practice for over forty-five years; he has owned several firms in several states, including Ohio and Virginia. His areas of specialization include large-scale planning and project management for golf courses, resort communities, parks, and recreation facilities. He has served as associate professor of landscape architecture, and has lectured at colleges, universities, and conferences throughout the United States and overseas. A past president of ASLA National, he has served on ASLA committees and has been the Society's representative to the International Landscape Alliance.

Moderator: "How did you become interested in landscape architecture?"

Mortensen: "My father was an electrical engineer. . . . He and I were both good in math, and he wanted me to be an engineer as well. I hadn't really thought about a career, so I went over to look at the College of Engineering [at Ohio State] and decided I didn't want to be an engineer. But the School of Architecture was in the College of Engineering. So that seemed a pretty good out for me!

"The things we learned in late 1950s had nothing to do with landscape architecture today, but it was a beginning; it was what was happening. As I look over the room today, I think of how the

"This program is an exciting one. People from the older generation welcome the chance to talk about what we have done and do, and we all benefit from reviewing past careers.

While going over my career, thinking about what I'd done—and what I should have done—I recalled a similar ASLA meeting in, I think 1972 or 1973: The meeting was in Portland, we had some older people in the profession, champions in the profession, on a panel discussion. I was in charge of one panel with Hideo Sasaki and Friedberg and Halprin and Eckbo. We had a lunch to discuss the details beforehand and I thought, 'Holy Mackerel! I'm having lunch with these guys!'" —Robert Mortensen profession has evolved over the fifty years: mostly grays and blues and white shirts and ties, and serious close-cropped hair. . . . Over time, in the 1960s, that morphed into buckskins and beards, browns and tattered souls who looked like they'd come in from checking the trap lines!"

Mortensen discussed the role of change in our lives and careers. In his career counseling, he stressed the need for introspection as we build our careers, the need to know ourselves and understand our personality, then make changes accordingly. He described his own career path, starting businesses, merging with other firms, including the firm now known as Lewis Scully Gionet, Inc., and finally creating "Mortensen Associates" because ultimately he found he enjoyed being a sole practitioner best.

Mortensen: **"As landscape architects we deal with change, and the people we deal with in public meetings generally don't like change,** so we find ourselves needing to explain why we are making the changes."

He has also seen a real change in the public's understanding of the role of the landscape architect, from complete ignorance in the late 1960s, to today, when "people say 'oh wow!' and they cite some places that they've been and projects they are familiar with. . . . Many people don't understand the details of what we do; but today, I'm actually convinced that people who should know what a landscape architect does, do know what a landscape architect does."

When asked about retirement, Mortensen responded, "I think I retired about forty years ago, but I don't think I'll ever retire because I'm doing what I enjoy doing, and if I wasn't doing it, I don't know what I would be doing."

Moderator: "And your final words of advice?"

Mortensen: "It's important to give back to your profession. You're doing your job when it's your turn—when it's time, let the next group do it."

It's important to give back to your profession. You're doing your job when it's your turn—when it's time, let the next group do it. —Bob Mortensen

Darwina Neal

An ASLA Fellow, Darwina Neal was chief of Cultural Resources Preservation Services for the National Capital Region of the National Park Service (NPS). She managed the archeology, history, and architecture programs and served as a liaison between the NPS staff and other agencies and community groups working on planning and park design. She joined ASLA in 1965, and has been active at every level—local, national, and international. She was the first woman elected as ASLA president and has consistently represented ASLA at international bodies including the International Federation of Landscape Architects (IFLA) and the International Council on Monuments and Sites.

Moderator: "How did you become interested in landscape architecture?"

Neal: "I was brought up on a farm in northern Pennsylvania, a poultry, dairy chicken hatchery farm with the smallest federally licensed poultry processing plant in the country. I was really grounded from the beginning. I started working on the grounds around the house, and digging up wildflowers in the woods and planting them in shady areas around our house. At Penn State the horticulture program was located in the same building as the landscape architecture program . . . and I switched into landscape architecture. I have had no regrets since. I've been very happy being a landscape architect."

Neal described her first job offer at the National Park Service in 1965 as a GS-5 earning $5,590 per year. Neal was the third woman hired as a landscape architect at the NPS. Earlier, Kathryn Cochrane noted that she had initially been refused a job at the NPS after college. "We don't hire women as landscape architects," she was told. Three years later she tried again and was the first woman hired.

Like Cochrane, Neal worked on the First Lady's Beautification Task Force. **"Mrs. Johnson's adage was to 'plant masses of flowers where masses of people passed.'"** *Neal proceeded to design and review many Washington, DC spaces, like the Tulip Library, the White House gardens, Rock Creek Park, and the vice president's residence. Her work at Camp David included the introduction*

In 1972, Darwina Neal chaired a task force investigating the status of women in the profession, part of her considerable service to ASLA. The resulting report, entitled *Women in Landscape Architecture* was published in July 1973. The report found that 5 percent of ASLA members were women, and no women were teaching full time in schools of landscape architecture. Today, reflecting thirty-five years of progress, 34 percent of ASLA members are women; many women teach in landscape architecture programs; and thirteen schools of landscape architecture have female department heads. Many women are principals at large firms throughout the profession.

"[At Camp David] They built a small conference center that was poorly designed and wasn't draining properly. So I got the backhoe operator, Herman, to go into the woods with me and gather up rocks, set them naturally into the slope to disrupt the water flow near the conference building, then planted around them. Herman kept kidding that he'd never planted rocks before." —Darwina Neal

I have always seen landscape architecture as a living legacy. What we do lives on long after we create it; it doesn't matter if anyone knows we did it.—Darwina Neal

of native plantings in place of struggling lawns, and remedial drainage work. As she climbed the career ladder at the NPS, Neal gradually became responsible for several hundred circles, squares, and triangle parks in the L'Enfant plan, and for the historic parkways that bring people to the DC area. Speaking of her work on the Lyndon Baines Johnson Memorial Grove, Neal says she was "fortunate to work with landscape architect Meade Palmer—from the initial site selection through design and construction, to post-construction evaluation."

In 1989, Neal became chief of Design Services, which included design and construction document review for the later memorials such as the Vietnam and Korean War Memorials, the Women in Vietnam and Law Enforcement Officers Memorials, and the Frances Scott Key Memorial. Moving on to the position of chief of Cultural Resource Preservation Services in 1995, Neal's work moved into multidisciplinary programs in archeology, historic preservation, research, inventory and evaluation of cultural resources— HALS before its time.

On the importance of mentorship in our profession, Neal thanked Ray Freeman for encouraging her to get involved in ASLA—and for "serving as both a role model and mentor to me—as he did for many landscape architects. **It is important to give back by mentoring other landscape architects**, and I continue to do this even as I am a vice president of ASLA."

Moderator: "Any final words of advice?"

Neal: "I have always seen landscape architecture as a living legacy. What we do lives on long after we create it; it doesn't matter if anyone knows we did it. . . . No matter how good a design is, it's no good unless (1) it can be constructed, (2) it can be used, (3) it can be maintained at the level of maintenance it can realistically be expected to receive. Too many people make mistakes in that regard."

"In order to survive, we need hope, flexibility, and a sense of humor."

Session Two: A Life of Public Service

Moderator: Karen Kumm Morris, ASLA

Edited by Adele N. Ashkar, ASLA

Participants:

Donovan E. Hower, FASLA, *past director of the Veterans Administration's Land Management Services, was in charge of site work for hospitals and cemeteries.*

Ralph J. D'Amato, Jr., ASLA, *earned a BS in landscape architecture at the University of Massachusetts in 1959. He practiced landscape architecture for over forty years, the last twenty-two years with the Veterans Administration, where he designed over sixty-eight cemeteries.*

Joseph Kondis, ASLA, *earned a BA in landscape architecture at Penn State University. He joined Maryland Parks and Planning as landscape architect and rose to be chief of the Maryland Parks Department's Engineering and Design Division during the 1970s and 1980s.*

Moderator: "About 12 percent of the Potomac Chapter membership work in the public sector; they work at all levels of the public sector and responsibilities vary greatly. What motivated you to choose public sector landscape architecture work?"

Hower: "I was born and raised on a dairy farm in Pennsylvania; my mother was a teacher. My father never graduated from high school, but was first to run contour farming on his dairy farm, and the first to have a Holstein herd of cows. Because my dad never got around to planting flowers on the farm, my mother would say to me, 'Don, you're going to go to Penn State and come home and landscape my house.' And that's what happened. After the [military] service, I went to Penn State. . . . I had enrolled in an agricultural engineer curriculum for the first year and it took me a year to figure out that I was in the wrong curriculum! You all have first year and it took me a year to figure out that

You all have the responsibility to mentor our young people, sell them on landscape architecture and get them headed in the right direction.
—Donovan E. Hower

I was in the wrong curriculum! You all have the responsibility to mentor our young people, sell them on landscape architecture and get them headed in the right direction.

"Now, I brag every day about my career; and when you can brag about your career, you're in the right one. After Penn State I went into a design/build organization, where the man was also a landscape architect, but he would have me design a landscape for a school or factory and then say 'Pick your crew to do the planting, I'll get the plants, and you go out and put those plants in.'

"When I applied for a Grade-9 position at the Veterans Administration, they looked at my experience where I worked with a crew to plant what I had designed—and said it didn't qualify. **But let me tell you, I learned more in my first three years as a design/build supervisor from my mistakes and successes, than during any other three years in my whole career!**"

D'Amato: "I also grew up on a farm. Never heard of a landscape architect in Massachusetts in the early 1950s. I just knew I didn't want to continue in farming. My grandfather would come every spring and prune and being the oldest kid, I picked up the branches after him. I liked that idea, so I figured I would be a landscaper with a truck and shovels. Then someone said, 'You should learn how to design what you are going to do.' So I enrolled in ornamental horticulture at UMASS. The professor who was head of landscape architecture also oversaw ornamental horticulture and swung me over to that. I also went into a design/build firm after school, and it was best education I ever had.

"I worked with the Highway Department through Lady Bird's beautification era, then went with the National Cemetery Administration and eventually joined the Veterans Administration, working on hospitals for a few years under Don Hower. Being that I had a large family to support, I had a practice on the outside also, doing residences, commercial buildings, and private cemeteries. As time went on, I did over one hundred private cemeteries, and am still doing private cemeteries since retiring from the VA. The ability to serve veterans was very important. And, yes, I did a few pet cemeteries too!"

Kondis: "I attended Penn State University in the 1950s on the Korean War GI Bill, with the idea of studying engineering. Because I'd worked as a landscape designer with the Army Corps of Engineers, I took engineering drafting courses at Fort Belvoir in 1949–50, so I could get a job when I got out of the military, because my brother told me long ago, 'There aren't going to be any more wars!'

"In 1949, I had asked my recruiting sergeant what he could do for me, and told him I could draw. He showed me the engineering drafting course at Fort Belvoir, but of course I had to enlist and go through basic training first. Next thing I know I was in California on a Sunday afternoon, June 25, 1950, and the Korean War broke out. Military being what it is, they sent me to Okinawa first with aviation engineers to extend airfields. They weren't using me for what I was trained to do, so I asked my First Sergeant, 'Can you send me where they can use me?' And of course that was Korea. I learned one thing—to keep my mouth shut! I stopped in Tokyo on my way to Korea and saw some very beautiful Japanese gardens, I saw General MacArthur, then Korea, and was with the aviation engineers, designing or improving existing airfields.

"After the war, I enrolled in engineering at Penn State, but a course called calculus turned me into a landscape architect! It was Greek to me! . . . I came to the Park and Planning Commission in Silver Spring because I'd heard they were looking for landscape architects. I got the job and stayed there until 1985. I retired as chief of Engineering and Design Division. . . . The park system was starting up from scratch. John P. Hewitt, director of Parks, hired me; that guy knew how to direct parks. He built Montgomery County's parks. Wheaton Regional Park was one of the first two regional parks in the Washington regional area."

Creating the Japanese Fragrance Garden at Brookside

"Years ago, in Rockville, the County was expanding its landfill sites, and planned to take over a portion of the Gilbert Gude tree nurseries. U.S. Representative Gude approached the County's Parks and Planning Commission and offered to dig up, move, and plant the trees if Brookside Gardens could accommodate them. Outcome: The Gude Garden at Brookside Gardens. When Hans [Hanses] made changes to the Japanese Fragrance Garden, he was out there making changes *on* the ground, not with a pencil! When you see the Japanese Garden, I say 'only in America can a German landscape architect win a White House award designing a Japanese garden.'"—Joe Kondis

Moderator: "How did Brookside Gardens get started?"

Kondis: "There was a lot of other development in the park before the Brookside concept. Wheaton Regional Park is roughly five hundred acres. Brookside Gardens came along with the development of the Brookside Nature Center . . . **I did the first Brookside Garden Master Plan, approved on June 16, 1965.** But I told my boss that to make it work we'd have to find the right landscape architect with the right skills and capabilities to work on this and nothing else. Hans Hanses had been working for a consultant engineering firm doing work for us. When I looked at this work I thought, 'We've got the right person if we can get him,' . . . Hans Hanses won four different White House awards, working with three different First Ladies. . . . Hans Hanses took my original 1965 Master Plan and took care of the plantings, producing the gardens which Brookside are today."

Moderator: "What are you now doing with your skills in architecture?"

Hower: "**I retired twenty-six years ago, in 1982. Then I really started to be a landscape architect!** One of the most exciting things I'm doing now [relates to when] I was appointed by Bruce Babbitt to a commission to save fifteen Civil War battlefields in the Shenandoah Valley. Three had already disappeared to development, so Congress passed a bill [that authorized the] purchase and preservation of the remaining Shenandoah Battlefields. . . . I was appointed [to the commission] from the McDowell County–Highland County area, near the West Virginia border area, and I've received several awards—as a Yankee!—from the United Daughters of the Confederacy. . . . It's one of the most fascinating things I've done. I chair the Resource Management Committee: We buy battlefields, then decide how to develop the lands we acquire so they can be showcased. It's a lot of fun."

D'Amato: "After I retired from the government, I kept working with my private cemetery clients and I continue to work with them. With cemeteries, you fill up the areas you have, then you need to expand. Also, I'm now an expert witness in cemetery law cases, testifying as to whether what they've done to correct problems is what should be done. Some places haven't surveyed their cemeteries properly, and we have discovered cemeteries where people are buried every which way and it has to be straightened out. I've been involved with some heavy-duty class action lawsuits and still working overseeing corrections."

Moderator: "Is there still a place for the public sector landscape architect, given that so much work is contracted out?"

D'Amato: "Yes there is. Ever since I've been in the government, since 1961, they've been trying to cut the numbers of government employees. It was done in the VA to a drastic extent. When we [Hower and D'Amato] started in 1970, we had three hundred and some people working in-house and we could design in-house start to finish, with people in every discipline that you'd need. . . . Then they cut back on what we could do and we reviewed consultants' plans, but we still had all disciplines in-house to review consultants' plans. Don [Hower] was instrumental in getting landscape architects to be the prime consultants on cemetery development programs, a tough accomplishment in a place full of architects and engineers! We had as primes some of the best firms in the country, but somebody needs to tell them how a hospital or cemetery works.

"But I'm sorry to say that by the time I left in 2001 . . . there were so few in-house people left to review plans that **we were hiring consultants to review the work of other consultants**, which made no sense because they also didn't know much about how hospitals and cemeteries work. **Also, landscape architects make the best project managers.** We know how to deal with the egos of architects and engineers and to try to get them together. That's all I did the last nine years I was [at the VA] and it worked pretty good."

ASLA's Potomac Chapter in 1961

"Through a series of interesting coincidences, in 1961 I came to DC for a job with the DC Federal Highway Department, and also started attending ASLA meetings. This is incredible to see so many landscape architects at this meeting! When I started in 1961, there weren't that many. At least 50 percent of the twenty to thirty people who came to [ASLA] meetings were government workers. Ray Freeman was a major force; we had a gentleman, Wilbur Simonson, who designed the Blue Ridge Parkway. Landscape architects did major things back then, but you didn't hear about it as they worked with the engineers. Now there are more private landscape architects in the area, and I think it's great. But getting in the public sector was the best thing I ever did."

—Ralph D'Amato, Jr.

Participants:

James van Sweden, FASLA, is a graduate of the University of Delaware and is credited (with partner Wolfgang Oehme) as author of the "New American Garden" style. The work of their firm: Oehme, van Sweden & Associates, includes among others, the World War II Memorial in Washington, DC; the Chicago Botanic Garden; and projects for the US State Department in Kabul, Afghanistan. He is the author of four major books, and is a frequent lecturer and guest on radio and television shows.

Florence Everts, ASLA, is a native of Sydney, Australia, and holds a graduate degree in anthropology. As a member of the United Nations Secretariat (India and Pakistan) and with her husband in the US Foreign Service, she had the opportunity to practice abroad in Iran, Pakistan, and Bangladesh. Her previous works include the US Embassy in Pakistan and site studies for the then-US Embassy in Beijing, China. Her work has been recognized internationally with numerous awards for historic preservation and design.

J. Brooks Breeden, FASLA, is a native of North Carolina and taught at Ohio State University for more than thirty years. His academic interests included promoting computer-aided instruction in tutoring and supplementing teaching processes. His work with site engineering tutorials for landscape architecture students has led to the development of LARCH Software.

Moderator: "Can landscape architects make an impact on environmental issues?"

van Sweden: "It begins in everyone's own garden. If you look at the landscape around any American city, there are no gardens. There is no love for the land. It's all lawn—using the worst material anyone can use. . . . It's lawn, noise, and total boredom. . . . No one is doing anything with their land. It begins with educating people about what can be done with their own land. I was in Loudoun County and was horrified looking at these McMansions where cows used to graze. I've since come to think of the McMansion as immense cows grazing. **We also have clients who are buying the mansions and tearing them down and bringing back the land.** We need to encourage people to enjoy their own space and begin using it."

Breeden: "Protecting the health, safety and welfare is a real ally for this profession for doing good things. We need to look at how that type of action can make us more visible and vocal."

Everts: "Think of the open core of the National Mall. In 2001, the National Capital Planning Commission designated that the central reserve area [be free] of future memorials. . . . Yet here we are in 2008, and we will be having an underground Visitor's Center for the Vietnam Memorial, and it will cause tremendous pedestrian activity. Why do we need a Visitor's Center?"

Moderator: "Very few landscape architects write. How to get past this impasse of people not writing? . . . How do we get more landscape architects writing?

van Sweden: "Writing is a very special talent and not everyone can do it. In my case I was able to get a fabulous publisher and great editor, Jason Epstein, who encouraged me to write. **Also, you need to have a cause that you believe in; then the writing comes naturally.** That's probably the key. You can learn to write, but nobody likes to do it that I know. It's tough and takes discipline."

Breeden: "Writing takes criticism. Nobody likes to have an editor tell you [that you] have written a bad paragraph! You'd just as soon not do it!"

Everts: "Landscape architecture needs an Ada Louise Huxtable—the fearless architecture critic who went to New York in the 1960s—her pieces were written with such directness and clarity. She had the politicians, bureaucrats, architects all ducking whenever one of her pieces came out. It shows the impact an urban critic can have; a good critic can lead the blind public to what is good. Her influence was enormous. We need a spokesman who can write like that!"

Moderator: "Computer-aided design and construction—landscape architects dragged their feet when it came to the computer, behind the architects and engineers. . . ."

Breeden: "The computer revolution is a mixed blessing. Why bother to letter like Frank Ching when you can just use the Tekton font? It's important for a landscape architect to be able to do quick sketches and drawings by hand that don't look like they've been done by a young child. Computers don't do quick sketches and thinking very well. They do final drawings well. It's wonderful to have a CAD machine instead of a pin-register bar, and before that, sepias, which shrank and stretched, and never aligned properly. CAD does straight lines very, very well. . . . Landscape architects used to love these rubber snakes they would use to lay in curves. I used to say if I see one of those on your desk, I'll wrap it around your neck! . . . **Tools change, but the built project is the goal**—to get the client convinced you've got the answers he needs, to get him to go ahead with it, and to construct it, to build your idea.

"**I think the cell phone has had more of an impact on the practice of landscape architecture profession than the computer,** because you can call into the office while out in the field. A GPS system that can be carried around in the pocket has had more of an impact, but they're all tied into computers. . . .

"Landscape architects didn't create Pentel pens and Magic Markers. They were created for writing on boxes so it wouldn't come off in the rain; but we picked them up and began to use them creatively. . . . Only recently when Autodesk came out with AutoCAD did we begin to see programs like LandCAD and others that dealt with the specific needs of landscape architecture."

Moderator: "What's the downside of the computer revolution?"

Everts: "The loss of elegant drafting; so many works of art were produced in offices and the quality of the work may vanish because students are now working on the computer."

Breeden: "There have been lots of changes in the thirty-five years since I started at Ohio State: we had a room with a five-cent cup of coffee, and exhibits went up in the room. There was once a Frank Lloyd Wright drawing exhibit and a faculty member had been to Taliesin and told the story of another faculty member who had gone out [to work with Wright] and Wright said, 'What am I going to do with you?' He was told to 'Trace the Robie House, you'll learn something.' He was infuriated, but he learned something. **You can't trace the Robie House on a computer and learn what you can by hand.**"

van Sweden: "When I get frustrated with these younger landscape architects staring at a computer screen all day, I remember what is was like to change the scale of the drawing. It took three or four days or even a week; now it takes at most a minute. That has transformed our office and others. We still do hand drawings and renderings; we insist on it. **We do the plan on the computer and hand-color everything because that quality of the hand drawing makes the difference.**"

Moderator: "Are practitioners getting students with the training that they need?"

van Sweden: "I think we are now. About ten or twelve years ago I told someone at the University of Virginia that I would not interview another landscape architect unless they were computer savvy. But now everybody is educated on a computer—but we are still very careful to make sure that they can also draw. **We only hire people who can draw.**"

Breeden: "Fifteen years ago, it was hard to find students just out of school that had computer skills, but fifteen years ago there weren't many faculty who had computer skills to pass on to the students. Faculty were struggling like old dogs trying to learn new tricks. . . . I desperately feel universities need practitioners to work as adjunct faculty to give students a sense of reality about what's going on outside that they don't believe when they hear it from the faculty. But if business is good, practitioners don't have the time to teach, and if business is bad, practitioners have time to teach, but universities don't have funds to hire the practitioners!

"There is a constant conflict between human needs and environmental values. . . . We must ask ourselves: What can we do as landscape architects to solve these problems? We need to become proactive to make our voices heard. . . . Our editor [Bill Thompson] raises these issues cogently in *Landscape Architecture Magazine*. . . . Landscape architects should be writing articles and letters to the daily press and work on projects that can influence developers."
—Florence Everts

The loss of elegant drafting; so many works of art were produced in offices and the quality of the work may vanish because students are now working on the computer.—Florence Everts

"Practitioners want a student who understands how to fit into an office and what the office is doing, who understands design and theory, but also has some practical skills, so they will not be a loss to the firm for their first couple years. For students to receive training on how an office works, faculty needs to have some business experience. . . . Without PhDs, professors of landscape architecture get no respect. Why? Because teachers are expected to have PhD's [and] practical experience doesn't help you get academic tenure. . . . Yet, universities are pushing to hire PhDs.

"There are good teaching opportunities for those who graduate, get practical experience, then return to school to get a PhD. . . . A normal BS or BLA is geared to teaching the discipline's fundamentals and a master's . . . teaches research methods in your area and your thesis teaches you how to write. . . . Most landscape architects have not pursued PhD coursework, so they've never had to write at the PhD dissertation level. They've been split between doing a thesis at the master's level that has more PhD in it than it should have. The result is that a landscape architect has to go two or three years for a master's degree, while an engineer only goes one year for a master's degree, but five years for a PhD."

van Sweden: "When I'm asked by students if they should stay and get a master's, I tell people to just get out there and work and build to get the experience. I think you should not take the time to get a master's degree. It takes so long to get a body of work together and create a style of your own."

Breeden: "That's good advice, but [if everyone followed that advice] we would be completely without departments of landscape architecture in very short order. Universities don't want to hire someone to teach without at least a master's, and preferably a doctorate. **If you want to teach, you have to go to graduate school.** The best way is this: I worked six years before I went to graduate school. But the likelihood that you'll go back to school after you've been out working decreases dramatically with the time you've worked before you go back."

Moderator: "There are many people who graduate with landscape architecture degrees who have never planted a tree. . . . Are there some basic skills we'll have to go back and learn, like plants?"

Everts: "I think it's true, but it's always been true. In academic courses, plant identification is secondary, is unimportant. But it is very important indeed.

van Sweden: "Some landscape architects think it's beneath them to be gardeners. When Wolfgang and I started out as landscape architects we both wanted to garden more than anything else. I wanted to get out there and plant."

Moderator: "Marketing your own practice?"

van Sweden: "I never thought of myself as a marketer, but once I left city planning, at thirty years old, and began to work as a landscape architect, I found marketing really easy. **I really believed in my work, and it's easy to market something you believe in.** There are many marketing vehicles; you can write books, give speeches, and learn to create photos like a professional. . . . Getting published is key to a successful practice, as is public speaking. . . . Also, this is a very complicated profession. No one person can know everything. When Wolfgang Oehme and I became partners, he a horticulturalist and I an architect, that was great. Study more than one aspect of the profession. Learn as much as you can about the profession, including horticulture and landscape architecture. Do whatever it takes to know as much as you can about the field."

"I remember the first time Lewis Clarke brought into my class a Pentel pen—he'd gotten it in San Francisco and brought it back to Raleigh, North Carolina. All the class gathered around, asking, "What is that?" And he proceeded to do the most beautiful line work with it."—Brooks Breeden

"I think it's the horticulturalist aspect of our firm that catapulted us to a success far greater than anything we'd imagined. Plants are really important—we have to emphasize their study. In Germany the university requires that you work in nurseries a year or two before getting a landscape architecture degree. This is key."
—James van Sweden

Oehme, van Sweden | OVSLA.COM

The Federal Reserve
Washington, DC, 1978, 2004

For more than three decades, Oehme, van Sweden & Associates' (OvS) extensive knowledge of ecological processes and deep commitment to artistic execution has resulted in a strong sculptural relationship between architecture and landscape. OvS' appreciation of nature and its processes inspired the firm's widely recognized "New American Garden" style. This approach is based upon celebrating the seasonal qualities of the natural environment and driven by a deep understanding of natural science. The results are beautiful and practical: OvS landscapes require less maintenance, no pesticides, and limited water and fertilization. They continue to function as a vital component of existing eco-systems while serving the needs of people.

The firm's widely diversified mix of clients includes federal-government agencies such as the National Park Service, US Fish and Wildlife Service, US Department of State, Smithsonian Institution, Federal Reserve Board, American Battle Monuments Commission, and the National Arboretum as well as private institutions, universities, municipalities, private businesses, and estates.

The Federal Reserve
Washington, DC, 1978, 2004

Ronald Reagan Washington National Airport
Arlington, Virginia, 1996
Architect: Hartman-Cox Architects

National Association of Realtors
Corporate Headquarters
Washington, DC, 2004
Architect: Graham Gund Partnership

National Association of Realtor
Corporate Headquarter
Washington, DC, 200
Architect: Graham Gund Partnership

World War II Memorial
Washington, DC, 2004
Architects: Frederick St. Florian, Hartman-Cox

Embassy of Finland
Washington, DC, 1994
Architect: Heikkinen-Komoner

303 Waster Street
Washington, DC, 2001
Architects: Frank Schlesinger Associates, Handel Architects, LLP

3303 Waster Street
Washington, DC, 2001
Architects: Frank Schlesinger Associates, Handel Architects, LLP

Chesapeake Bay, Maryland, 2002
Architect: Sorg and Associates

Georgetown I
Washington, DC, 2002

Georgetown II
Washington, DC, 2003

UNITED STATES DEPARTMENT OF TRANSPORTATION HEADQUARTERS

WASHINGTON, D.C.

The United States Department of Transportation Headquarters was a development catalyst covering two city blocks in Southeast Washington DC. The design provides ample sidewalk and greenspace, and offers first flush stormwater catchment. Additional storm water benefit is attained via the largest extensive green roofs in Washington, DC on both buildings. A large brick plaza provides space flexibility for festivals, markets, outdoor movies, and the space is activated by a large double-sided water feature. Anacostia River access was also regained with the designed opening of Third Street SE.

°leeandassociates

Jeff S. Lee   FASLA

Bang Shon   ASLA
Rhonda Dahlkemper   ASLA
Lina Gong

Craig Atkins   ASLA
Adrienne McCray   ASLA
Eric Baugher   ASLA
Kwang Bin Lee   ASLA
Ben Tauber   ASLA

Gabriel Kruse   ASLA
Sorina Igreti   ASLA
Sara Downing   ASLA
Nick Haines   ASLA
Katharine Mitchell

[LAB]

LANDSCAPE ARCHITECTURE BUREAU

The Landscape Architecture Bureau [LAB] has gained a reputation for exploring the limits of design no matter the size, scope, or project resources, resulting in spaces that engage the senses and satisfy their users, creating places that are memorable and a credit to the community as a whole.

LAB's work fuses art, science, and stewardship, crafting designs that are imaginative and iconic. From the beginning, we work to identify a guiding concept, a strong, simple, clear idea. We implement this idea consistently throughout the project.

We have a responsibility both to steward the environment and to embolden and deepen the relationship between natural systems and the people on which they depend. LAB is committed to an expanded notion of sustainability, beyond simple environmental protection. We believe that only well-conceived, well-constructed places, made beautiful and inclusive of the people surrounding them, will be loved by their users sufficiently to make them sustainable.

1101 K Street NW

Stanford University Washington Center

Oliveros Residence

Diamond Teague Park

Ross Elementary School Playground

Oliveros Residence

Concord Residences

Concord Residences

Cady's Alley

On April 17, 2009, in celebration of National Landscape Architecture Month, Potomac Chapter members who are principals, directors or owners of their firms or agencies were invited to participate in public discussions surrounding their practice of landscape architecture. The result was a full-day symposium, featuring five round-table discussions, held at the Jack Morton Auditorium of The George Washington University in Washington, DC. Moderating the sessions were five young landscape architects from the Chapter. The following articles, prepared by the moderators, are highly abridged excerpts of the lively discussions of the day, which were often peppered with the personal experiences of the panelists.

Session One: Defining the Local Landscape

Moderator: Brandon Hartz, ASLA

Participants: Stephanie Bothwell, ASLA, Director, Center for Livable Communities, Washington, DC; Paul Dolinsky, ASLA, Chief, National Park Service Historical American Landscape Survey (HALS); Douglas A. Hays, ASLA, Michael Vergason Landscape Architects, Alexandria, Virginia; Brian P. Kane, ASLA, Principal, The Kane Group, LLC, Alexandria, Virginia; Robert B. Tilson, FASLA, President, The Tilson Group, Vienna, Virginia; and Guy Morgan Williams, ASLA, President, DCA Landscape Architects, Washington, DC

Moderator: "The panel's theme of 'Defining the Local Landscape' refers both to the literal and generic descriptions of 'landscape,' including the current economic landscape, the academic and ecological landscapes, and the myriad historical contexts that one must deal with regarding any site. What is your favorite local landscape and why?"

Dumbarton Oaks makes me ask, "How can I bring this sense to anything that I create as a landscape architect?"—Guy Williams

Brian Kane: "In an area with such breadth of landscapes, one of my favorite landscapes, because it teaches us many things about our region, is George Washington Memorial Parkway and Mount Vernon Highway. Both the landscape architect and non-landscape architect understands the story of Washington as this city on a river, built on a marsh, that is also recipient of waters coming from all over, from the Appalachians and Blue Ridge, as well as the tidal Chesapeake Bay."

Doug Hays: "That's the way I take people into the city, because this is the way you can see the beauty and the unfolding of the city, from the fall line all the way down into the center of the city. You see the evolution of the city from its pinnacle of the Washington Monument, and some nights you even see the lights on the Capitol Dome."

Paul Dolinsky: "Taking this as an opportunity to speak about historic preservation, I choose Dumbarton Oaks Park, at one point little known but becoming better known. Not the garden that we all know and love but the landscape behind the garden, below the famous garden, that really is the watershed for Wisconsin Avenue flowing down into Rock Creek Park. It's a heavily designed, naturalistic landscape—a series of waterfalls that manage the watershed, and a series of structures supporting the beautiful meadows that Beatrix Farrand created."

Moderator: "Do any of these landscapes reinforce the importance of your professional work?"

Guy Williams: "The first time I went to Dumbarton Oaks was in 1983, shortly after I moved here. It was very reaffirming, experiencing both the garden's level of detail and its simplicity. . . . How do you draw the essence of a space like that—whether doing a very detailed design or something simple—how do you create the essence of a sense of place that is enduring? Dumbarton Oaks makes me ask, 'How can I bring this sense to anything that I create as a landscape architect?'"

Stephanie Bothwell: "Everyday when I need to think about how to make a road or street I can always refer back to the plan of the city and think how does that apply to this new place, where we need to bring very successful, dense, sustainable, walkable communities, because the form of the city here has been able to accept so much change and growth over time—and has been such a great template."

Moderator: "Stephanie, in our previous conversations, you'd mentioned doing some work in regards to money being allocated from the Stimulus Bill. Would you like to comment on how funding is being allocated locally or about the types of work you've been doing?"

Stephanie: "It's difficult to know at this time what the Stimulus Bill's impact is going to be. If someone knows the answer, please tell me! This is an exciting time to be a landscape architect because these efforts that we've never had on the table before are now in front of us, and the implications are incredible. For example, how can we create livable communities along rapid rail lines? Where should the cities be? How should they grow? What should the landscape look like and what will the connective tissue look like along these corridors as they develop?"

Paul: "I'm the odd person out as a practicing federal landscape architect, particularly working with historical landscape architecture. Regarding the Stimulus Package, the Historical American Landscape Survey (HALS) is one of the original WPA programs created to employ unemployed landscape architects and architects to document the rapidly vanishing national resources in the 1930s. When HALS was created in 2000 . . . the mission was the same: to document rapidly vanishing or endangered landscape examples throughout the country. We have a student labor force, and traditionally when the economy is booming there are few student applicants for these jobs because they get internships with firms. This year we have eight hundred student applicants for this summer . . . a fact indicative of where things are in the market."

Moderator: "Paul, as the chief of our National Historic Landscape Survey, how do you feel about the treatment, particularly maintenance and/or restoration, of our historic landscapes?"

Paul: "It's extraordinary. Can it be better? Of course. But in the context of the vast amount of sites maintained and managed by the National Park Service, what's being done is extraordinary. . . . I was

"What has influenced the work? For me as a child growing up, my mother would routinely take me through Fort Myer, through Arlington National Cemetery, where we would watch caissons, read gravesites, and sit on the knolls and look down over the vista. Then we would cross the Memorial Bridge, pull the car up very near the Lincoln Memorial and sit on the steps of the Memorial looking out over the Reflecting Pond. At that time the Mall was very neglected, if you recall, but for me it was a glorious procession into the city, all made for me. It was an amazing thing for a child to wander in these landscapes and participate on a daily basis, thinking 'isn't life grand?'"

—Stephanie Bothwell

Most landscape architects look at a project top down, and most contractors look at a project from the bottom up — and at some point we come together to meet and finalize a project. I know that my experience thinking both ways has made it easier for me to converse with all parties on a project. —Rob Tilson

struck this morning that all the landscapes that people mentioned as particularly meaningful to them are historic landscapes. The methodology of documenting these sites properly is extremely important to follow methodically, with measured drawing, written history and large format photography, and then following that path through the cultural landscape inventory and landscape reports required by the NPS to get to the maintenance levels that you see undertaken. So, yes, I think we're doing an extraordinary job."

Moderator: "Paul's an insider who knows what goes into the maintenance and management activities of historic landscapes. For the rest of us, who view this issue through the media lens, all you really hear is negativity about how our historic landscapes are maintained. Can any of you comment on public perceptions of how our historic landscapes are maintained? Any unspoken rules whether it is ever okay to alter a historic landscape?"

Brian: "Based on my experiences in the design area, what I'm finding are fragmented historic landscapes, particularly as our areas have become suburbanized. We're left with pieces out in the counties beyond Washington that are remnants, old historic properties that were working farms or prominent families' houses. How do we work with what's left, and recognize the context around it? One of the first calls we have is for protection of natural resources, even ahead of the historic resources. So, is it possible to alter a historical landscape? Yes, but it requires a lot of research first to understand what was there historically prior to making first design moves, and this is an area that landscape architects can and should be involved in leading the initiative."

Stephanie: "Thinking back, again, to my experience visiting the National Mall and going to the museums, there were no places to go to the bathroom, and no places to eat. The city has addressed that over the last twenty years. . . . I think it was in the McMillan Plan that Olmsted drew beer gardens on the Mall, knowing that people want to gather in the nighttime in a safe and good way. We might not be proposing beer gardens, but one of the problems with a grown-up city is that people want to be out in the parks, to hear entertainment, to have refreshments, and want to stay up late and revel in the city. But I find more and more, with security swinging the cat, sidewalk cafes are very difficult to establish and keep. There are not enough of them to really maintain the nightlife of the city, which is just as important as the day life. **We need to grow up as a city; the parks need to be more flexible, and we need to do everything else that everyone else in the world does in parks, and think that that is okay—and safe—and not politically incorrect."**

Moderator: "Brian, since you have taught at the university level, and to those of you who have interns in your offices—what do you see as the strengths and weaknesses of students coming out of school today versus those in the past?"

Brian: "This is one of the best cities and regions in the nation to study landscape architecture at schools such as University of Maryland and Virginia Tech and GW. There's a wonderful emphasis in some of the technical courses on the relationship between land and water and hydrological processes, which are becoming more involved in landscape architecture. This is an example of the fact that students are really well prepared for the types of problems they will encounter once they've started to practice."

Doug: "I'm from the old school. How far we've come from working on linen to now, working on computers that generate all these fancy illustrations and views. What I see in the students coming out of school today is that they are so much more technically attuned to computers and the software that can be used to develop these things. However, **I do think that one of the things that [has] been lost amidst the new technology is the ability to draw,** and I know Michael [Vergason] and I both need to draw to figure out what we're going to be doing when we design stuff. We should try not to lose the skill of drawing in the profession."

Paul: "I recall when our office made the transition from . . . hand drawing to computer-aided drafting. Inevitably the people who were trained beautifully with engineering drawing and hand drawing and sketching translated that skill most effectively into exquisitely crafted computer-aided drafting projects. In reviewing these hundreds of applications now I see a loss of the craft of pencil on paper. The educational process lacks training for the artistic—and technical—aspect of the process, putting pencil to paper."

Moderator: "Are there any lessons you'd like to pass on to younger generations of landscape architects coming out of school?"

Guy: "**Nothing put to paper or in a design, compares to the ability to understand your clients, how to work with them, understand the contractors and the folks who do the work**. . . . Because of the wide variety of careers that landscape architects enter, the tools taught in school provide the technical ability; **but in order to be able to use that technical ability to bring designs and projects to fruition, it means you need to get down in the trenches working with the contractors.** What's key is understanding your clients, realizing that your best traits can be your worst traits, and really analyzing how to assemble the teams needed to really accomplish a project and make it a difference."

Rob Tilson: "What I've learned over the years as a landscape architect—wearing two hats as both landscape architect and a contractor—is that most landscape architects look at a project top down, and most contractors look at a project from the bottom up – and at some point we come together to meet and finalize a project. I know that my experience thinking both ways has made it easier for me to converse with all parties on a project, and think that if we all look more holistically at projects, we will have more successful projects."

This is an exciting time to be a landscape architect because these efforts that we've never had on the table before are now in front of us, and the implications are incredible.—Stephanie Bothwell

Session Two: The Importance, Identity, and Role of Today's Landscape Architect

Moderator: Sarah Story

Participants: Claire Bedat, ASLA, Landscape Architecture Bureau, Washington, DC; Stephen G. Gang, ASLA, The Lessard Group, Vienna, Virginia; Marsha A. Lea, ASLA, AECOM, Alexandria, Virginia; Joseph Plumpe, ASLA, Studio 39 Landscape Architecture, PC, Alexandria, Virginia; Charles H. Trace, Jr., ASLA, Trace Landscape Architecture, Inc., Washington, DC; and Michael Vergason, FASLA, Michael Vergason Landscape Architects, Ltd., Alexandria, Virginia

Landscape architects work with a variety of related professionals and also work for firms dominated by one of these other disciplines. The panel members were asked what changes they have seen in the way that other professionals view them and how landscape architects interact with those other disciplines. Are landscape architects taking on more of a lead role in projects? With landscape architects so often addressing the interface of structures with the site, are they well suited to take on this role? Are they taking on more of this role than in the past?

Steve Gang responded that he believes that "our education uniquely suits us for this role. I consider landscape architects as renaissance people, able to view the whole world as a global picture compared to looking only at individual pieces of the pie." He went on to describe his role as a landscape architect working in an architecture firm. He said that when he tells people "I'm a landscape architect, their jaws drop, asking, 'How can you know all that stuff in reference to how to put buildings together, how to put cities together, how to understand the different marketing components, engineering, legalese?' I think our role of handling all that [means that] . . . we are really geared for leadership roles."

Joe Plumpe noted that "over the past five to eight years, we have seen our project roles change from being in a support position . . . to taking on team leadership responsibilities, working with a number of consultants working under us" even if "the majority of us [are still] working within a larger team."

I can only encourage everyone to think more broadly out of the box than what we've been able to do in the past.—Michael Vergason

Michael Vergason summed up our role in this collaborative effort, saying, "we're in the jack-of-all-trade position. . . . [In school] what we learned was how to make things work—and to work well—both as to design, as well as when they get built. . . . Now is a fun time being a landscape architect. It's different than it used to be, compared to having been in a very supportive role in the 1980s. I can only encourage everyone to think more broadly out of the box than what we've been able to do in the past." He recalled the role of landscape architects in the distant past, "being the planners and leaders of the new towns. We'd lost that role in the mid-1900s, but now's our time to come back and take up where we left off back then. It's a very difficult situation to show that we can contribute more to a project than people think."

Claire Bedat offered, "We need to be inserting creative energy into the design charrette debate." She continued, "I emphasize that we have to be visible, challenge the players around the table—including the client—and just open up a real creative dialogue."

The panel was asked about their experience in regards to the timeliness of their involvement as part of the collaboration.

Marsha Lea felt "we tend to work with clients who allow us to work in a collaborative fashion early on, getting involved in helping to formulate the early decisions . . . we look for opportunities to continue to work with those clients who understand our role and when to involve us," but conceded that "we occasionally get involved in a project where it might be too late to effect change if change is necessary. It's all about working with who you're comfortable with—someone who recognizes the skill set you bring to the table."

Charles Trace disagreed. "A collaborative team requires sufficient research and analysis in the very beginning of the project, and we're often brought in too late—to do the green roof, to do the public space—and it's not well incorporated. . . . **We would approach problem-solving quite differently if we were involved in a project from the outset.**"

Ms. Bedat challenged, "I think we should ask ourselves, 'Why are we being brought in too late?' It is the perception of the others that we are not participating at the same level. So how do we start changing the cards at this level? That's the question to ask for both the student and practitioner, how to re-educate the population that we're working within to make sure that we are brought in at the right time. How do we do that?"

One area where Mr. Vergason had noted landscape architects gaining prominence was in the Leadership in Energy and Environmental Design (LEED) program. He described "other consultants [coming] to us to discuss how we can get the certification level that they're looking for—[we're] not just staying off on the sidelines, just doing tree planting plans."

Mr. Plumpe echoed this sentiment saying that "especially with the LEED movement, [clients] are trying to get us involved sooner because we bring a lot to the table. **We are educating our client base that we're not just the guys with the plant list any more.** We're the guys who can help you get the project through." He also noted that many jurisdictions are now requiring some level of LEED certification and surmised, "I think things will only get better."

Mr. Vergason also found that, "in all areas there has been an increased awareness of the talent we bring to projects, and there is nowhere that we can be more effective than working through the people in the public sector because they can be effective allies in bringing good design to a project at the right time."

Mr. Gang also observed, "one of the great advantages is that landscape architects have been placed in positions of influence in the public review process. Landscape architects are in positions from a politician to [a person] reviewing plans," where they can be an "ally who understands what you're trying to do."

Considering media such as Landscape Architecture Magazine, *blogs like* DCMUD *and* Pruned, *and* HGTV, *the moderator asked how the media coverage of the profession had changed over the span of their careers and if it is accurate in how it portrays the role of landscape architects.*

I emphasize that we have to be visible, challenge the players around the table—including the client—and just open up a real creative dialogue.—Claire Bedat

Mr. Trace began a discussion of a recent article in the *Washington Post* critiquing the design of the Eisenhower Memorial. "I think it's interesting—and disturbing—that many architects are winning these memorial designs, not landscape architects." Furthermore Mr. Trace observed, "[The *Post* talks] about landscape architects designing benches, water features—but I think this is very interesting because the evolution of landscape does need to change. The article goes on to discuss the need for interactive design, digital design. . . . Rather than relying just on static elements, but including an interactive element."

Mr. Trace then turned his attention to nonprint media. "HGTV, even though it has brought attention to the profession, does a disservice to the rigor, the research, the analysis—all the many things we put into the design, none of which is even touched on by HGTV."

"What's good about HGTV," Mr. Plumpe weighed in, "is that it educates people about plant material at a basic level, but it would also be interesting to have a program that talks about what landscape architects really do."

Ms. Bedat called for "including an element of glamour in any program . . . I think that when we expose what we do, we blend in with work itself. We are not standing out . . . perhaps HGTV is not the right medium for us, but we certainly should use this medium to promote what we do."

Citing the aforementioned *Washington Post* article, Mr. Vergason suggested that "the problem is this definition of 'good work'—that is implicit, if not explicit in the article—that 'good work' needs to break new ground, and I don't believe that. In fact, I think that's a burden."

Mr. Gang returned to the dynamic and flexible roles landscape architects take on—this time as a challenge. "One of the disadvantages of our profession, in portraying it to the media, is that we're so spread out. There are so many aspects of our profession . . . landscape architects work for a variety of firms. So when we present ourselves to the media, which aspect are we presenting?"

Mr. Trace brought the discussion back to *Landscape Architecture Magazine*. He expressed his desire to see it "evolve into more than just a trade magazine," and suggested "adding a bit of glamour and glossiness . . . because there's a lot of verbiage in *Landscape Architecture*." He'd like to see certain issues addressed, such as "How is the design landscape changing today? Are we designing spaces today the same way as in the past?" He felt that a failure to accurately answer some of these questions is "why architects are getting many of the public space commissions. . . . That's the issue, because we can contribute much more than that to a project."

Ms. Bedat noted that most of her "influence and perception comes from *Dwell* and *Metropolis* magazines." She emphasized that "we need to tune into this world outside our profession as well."

The panelists were asked how they are using new technologies in the design process. Furthermore, they were asked how younger people are using these skills and how this informs their design process.

Ms. Lea responded, "We're designing faster. The three-dimensional programs are wonderful for what they let you see quickly; but it's also easier to copy and not think about what you're drawing, so suddenly you can have a planting plan that has trees all over it. **Especially the younger designers are very capable graphically, but they are not sitting back and thinking about what they are creating as often as they should.**"

Mr. Gang saw technology as a "plus" because "you can understand things so quickly . . . if clients come in who don't like what we've done, almost instantly we can change things around for them . . . we can show them quickly what their idea would look like. . . . On the other hand, drawing is a lost art. Every youngster who comes in doesn't know how to hand draw. . . . Even though a computer can look at the whole universe, your eye goes to one point and somehow the whole big idea of the story you're trying to tell is lost. So the new technology has both its advantages and disadvantages."

Ms. Bedat noted, "Having the advantages of this new technology doesn't take away from the need to get out of the office, to get out on the site and see where you are working," but she added, "we need to embrace what [technology] does for us—and expand on this."

"If there's any single piece, [over the span of my career], that represents a sea change in how we do our work, it is the digital medium in all its aspects: research, communication, and presentation, including verbal, graphic, and written." But he noted the challenge that technology presents. "It also exhausts me because it changes the pace of everything we do. It improves not only the accuracy but [also] the efficiency of what we do. I'd like to think we can take advantage of the time saved . . . to reflect on what we're doing."—Michael Vergason

Mr. Plumpe shared a related observation, "What we're finding is that clients actually prefer the hand drawing and hand rendering style, going full-circle from the 1980s when everything was done by hand. . . . These are developers, so maybe there is hope that hand-drawing will come back."

Mr. Trace was emphatic about technology, saying, "It is a plus, plus, plus! . . . With access to digital information, Google, etc., there should be no question unanswered in the design process before construction. One can get so much information—and get it quickly—that I think it's critically important. Your ability to problem-solve, to produce and evaluate alternatives, is amazing—and one could not do that previously."

Mr. Vergason elaborated, "**The process of drawing allows you to refine your skills of perception, of judgment.**" Specifically, he referred to AutoCAD as an example. Mr. Vergason acknowledged, "[my colleague] Doug's work in AutoCAD has the same quality as the work that he does by hand. So I think drawing is holding the talents we have for aesthetic judgment regarding proportion, size—everything we do."

Mr. Gang had a different perception. "Some people feel comfortable with hand-drawing, others with the computer. Drawing just gives us another option for how we present that thought process and it's the thought process that gets us to a solution as quickly as possible."

The panel was asked for final thoughts.

Mr. Vergason was philosophical, stating, "We do a number of fifty-year master plans, and I am always impressed by the idea that it's impossible to imagine what life will be like in fifty years. But then you look back fifty years . . . and it astounds me [the] speed with which that time passed . . . I remember temporary buildings around the Washington Monument, so the idea that there's this perception of time—feel the present, look to the future, reflect on the past. But also that there is an incredible urgency with everything we do. So my overriding comment is that we should exercise a great deal of patience with everything we do because these things happen so fast in the end."

Session Three: A Critical Look at Today's Sustainability

Moderator: Matthew Sellers

Participants: Lindsey W. Baker, ASLA, LWB Design, LLC; Dennis B. Carmichael, FASLA, AECOM, Alexandria, Virginia; Y. H. Connie Fan, ASLA, Lewis Scully Gionet, Inc, Vienna, Virginnia; Jonathan Fitch, ASLA, Landscape Architecture Bureau, Washington, DC; Joan Honeyman, ASLA, Jordan Honeyman Landscape Architecture, LLC, Washington, DC; Mark X. LaPierre, ASLA, LaPierre Studio, LLC, Alexandria, Virginia; Robert M. McGinnis, ASLA, AECOM, Charlottesville, Virginia

Moderator: "Our topic is Sustainability. We'll be discussing the impact on your design process and how it's evolved, the current state of implementing these principles, and the future of sustainable design. Joan, ten to fifteen years ago would sustainability have been as high on your list of priorities as it is today?"

Joan Honeyman: "Sustainability has been around for quite a long time, especially in Europe, but we came into this design thinking primarily over the past ten years; it seems like more forward thinking has come about as we've become more energy-conscious. My practice has been working to position ourselves to address issues such as water conservancy, plant growth, and sustainability of the land so that landscapes can be carried on into the future."

Dennis Carmichael: "I disagree a little. I think this happened over one hundred years ago when the profession was founded. It's at the core value of landscape architecture. It's what we do and who we are and we need to take credit for it. **As landscape architects we should own sustainability.**"

Rob McGinnis: "In my view as a preservation specialist, the other aspect of sustainability that is changing is an expansion of how sustainability is viewed. For clients like the National Park Service that's not an issue, but outside those types of agencies, looking at cultural sustainability . . . beyond global warming issues, has been around in pockets, but is certainly now changing for us in a broader sense."

Jon Fitch: "There's a difference in the emphasis depending on the kind of practice and projects. To the extent we are doing large-scale projects on which we are the prime consultants, and in which the interventions on the land are done in a landscape context, then our care and stewardship becomes critically important. When your work is, like ours, almost entirely highly urbanized, the impact of our work is no less, but is overshadowed by the importance of the care with which the buildings around us are made. This is not to say that what we do is unimportant—the moon is beautiful; but when the sun comes out the moon is less visible. But that doesn't make the moon less beautiful."

Dennis: "Either I don't understand what you're saying, or I totally disagree. As a landscape architect I can find organic connection to the earth, the setting I am a part of, in any environment you put me in. So, if I find a tree on a hundred-acre site, or a tree suffering on Pennsylvania Avenue, it needs the attention of a person who understands those organic systems. And, isn't that what the sustainability issue is about?"

Jon: "Which is exactly what I was saying."

Dennis: "Maybe the common link is a cultural connection, and as landscape architects, don't we need to understand and encourage that cultural connection to our organic environment whether we're in a city or in a green environment?

Jon: "Again, that's clearly very important to all of us, and the one tree that you find on the corner of Twenty-first and H is every bit as important as one tree on a hundred acres in George Washington National Forest."

Dennis: "Our challenge is to show how that one tree downtown is important to downtown urban situations. That's what stewardship is about."

Jon: "If in fact trees all over the city are planted in an execrable fashion, which in fact they are, and they all die within ten or fifteen years, which is basically what happens, and if the water does not infiltrate, as hardly ever happens, it would not change the environmental impact of the city of Washington very much. It might have some environmental impact, but it's not anything as important as if all buildings in the city had triple-paned glass, or all of them had high-energy furnaces and air conditioners."

Lindsey Baker: "I think it's a mindset; going back to what Dennis said, for landscape architects, stewardship of the land is at our core. . . . We have to be more conscious of sustainability and what that means for a particular project. It could be very small, could just be responsible plant material, being noninvasive; it could be concern about saving water. It could go from a large project to a small project, but **sustainability is mainly a mindset and people are more aware of that.**"

Joan: "We all have to be stewards. But the message wasn't out there ten years ago. Now, it's a matter of getting people to understand why they have to be sustainable, not just on big sites, but more so on urban sites where people have to understand the systems."

Connie Fan: "What's misleading right now is that people tend to think landscape architects only plant trees, mow lawns, cure any disease that your shrubs may have. We actually do way more than that. Even in an urban setting. I've seen jobs in DC where people try to capture water runoff from the sidewalk, which to me is very proactive. Rather than seeing that little bit of water go into the gutter, people are making an effort to capture that water."

Moderator: "On sustainability, where are we playing the leadership role that we should? Where could we be doing better?"

Dennis: "I don't think we are leaders; we should be. I've been scratching my head to figure out why we're not leaders. In 1991 the architects stopped doing 'entertainment architecture' and became the sustainable guys. In one year, just like that. They stole our thunder. And we've been struggling to get it back. And I think part of it is that we are a very humble profession. Architects build objects that in many cases control landscapes. We're a bit more maternal and nurturing of the environment and how we think about the land. So therefore we don't blow our own horn."

Sustainability is mainly a mindset and people are more aware of that.—Lindsey Baker

Rob: "We may not have done a good job selling this point on our own but this issue has resonated in recent years. I talk to a lot of people who aren't architects or landscape architects and we are now viewed as critical by many people. That wasn't the view ten years ago. They may misunderstand what we do, but somehow they do instinctively understand that we have some sort of important role to play in this whole broad spectrum of global climate change. **I can't tell you what green roofs have done for us—it's amazing.**"

Joan: "This makes me think of LEED and how LEED got started and how LEED is mostly architectural. We don't have a lot of points in LEED. I'm wondering how do we move past our little section and points that we get in LEED to a more prominent position? Being humble is great, but we're not out there enough."

Dennis: "In 2006, when I was president of ASLA that was an issue that was a great frustration—that one could get a LEED-certified building with a terrible landscape, and you could still get certified. So our membership decided 'Why couldn't you get a LEED-certified landscape?' So we've initiated the Sustainable Sites Initiative, which is to get at the core of that problem, and to bring that body of knowledge into the LEED process in a more robust way. It's been about four years. But you have to have the research and the correct benchmarking done at an academically peer-reviewed level to really have the impact and have a true validity. So, it will be another couple years before we can say that a landscape is LEED-certified."

Lindsey: "I want to return to Rob's point that now we're being more respected. I think that's maybe in the DC area, because I'm trying to break into the Cleveland market, and it's a totally different perspective. Landscape architects don't get the same acknowledgment, or even awareness. There's a big difference. We're very lucky here in the DC area. We have so many prominent landscape architects, people to look up to, and we can make our voices heard. But it is in other places we still need a lot of work."

Moderator: "This brings us to talking a bit more about implementing these practices in our work. Since we're already on the topic, what have been your experiences with LEED?"

Connie: "In terms of implementation, what I perceive is that there are quite a few hurdles related to technology and products available. For example, in the case of pavement, a lot of you know that concrete and asphalt are somewhat permeable, but research also shows that those pavements tend to require a lot of maintenance because the holes get plugged up. . . . We're still in a lot of the test and trial process. So as designers we definitely want to be in the forefront as leaders using materials that are recyclable and sustainable but in the meantime be willing to step in when things don't work out as they should and be willing to admit mistakes."

Moderator: "Is it important that Landscape Architects become LEED accredited?"

Dennis: "It's a good marketing tool, but also important to show that you are a part of the club, which is the overall design community. **That's the standard, so for better or for worse, that's where we need to be.** I would acknowledge that there are only a few points that landscape architects contribute to a LEED project, but what I found in my experience is that when we're at the table with all the other design professionals we can help influence and help make decisions by the group to make it better. As a profession we're a little more willing to think outside the box, and push things to new places. I think we should be part of it."

Mark LaPierre: "There's an objectification that happens with what we face and, as much as I support what Dennis says in respect to LEED, I think there is a perpetuation of the sensibility in our current culture that landscaped things are just these objects and we plug them into our LEED formula and it's all good."

Rob: "As a preservation specialist, we have been sustaining good design. I'm working on a pro bono project in Richmond, the Rice House, which is a Neutra-designed house that looks like it should be sitting in the desert, but sits above the James River. It's 1960s vintage. **It really is about**

"There is another expanded notion of sustainability that is absolutely part of the process in Europe that is not part of the process here. If a project is not loved, then it will not be sustained. If it's not great, it doesn't matter what the soils are: it will not be sustainable. And that is not now and, as far as I can tell, is not going to be part of what the public here uses to judge whether a project is sustainable. This is not the case in Europe because all those projects have to go through a public review not only of the equivalent of their LEED points, but address "Is this a great project?" And if it's not, you have to go back and redesign it."—Jon Fitch

I can't tell you what green roofs have done for us—it's amazing. Just that one piece has resonated with people who have no idea of what landscape architecture is about.—Rob McGinnis

sustaining culture and not just about high design. I think there's a model for sustaining the role of good design. . . . With LEED, you can tear down a historically significant building to put up a LEED-certified structure. But it's interesting that through that lens of how preservation relates to sustaining culture you begin to get at this issue that having that maternal instinct for caring and nurturing the design is critical to sustaining the design, or else it would just eventually be torn down and that's a waste."

Moderator: "Let's talk about the future. Where do we move forward to improve our position and improve sustainability in our products? Further out, how far is the sustainable movement really going to go?"

Dennis: "**Sustainability is not a fad and it has never been a fad. The word may be 'faddish,' but the message has never been. That also means it is never going to go away.** It simply has gotten more media play and, I think, a sense of urgency. I don't think we have to compromise high design. . . . We have to do both, and we have to make it affordable to do so that it becomes inevitable that it's not a choice, not something that you're seeking or that you're trying to convince people about, but that it instead becomes the way we do our business. If we do that as a profession, we will prosper as a result."

Jon: "I think it has everything to do with what we aspire to. Not everything we do will be remarkable; falling slightly short of that is better than not trying and coming up with something that does not do us or the culture proud. . . . We have to be able to look clearly at what we do to say 'that's great' and 'that stinks.' None of our work will be sustainable if we can't do that."

Mark: "Maybe it's great because it's durable, because it's still there, and it's still there because the culture cares. If we're going to sustain ourselves as a profession in an ever-urbanizing world with diminishing natural resources, then it behooves us to become more problem solvers in the broader sense, so that we're not just organically based, but also systems-based. But we do have to sustain the sensibility that all products, all things that shape our culture do come ultimately from a finite organic world."

Session Four: The Perception of the Landscape Architect

Moderator: Curt Millay, ASLA

Participants: Roger Courtenay, FASLA, AECOM, Alexandria, Virginia; Lisa E. Delplace, ASLA, Oehme, van Sweden & Associates, Inc., Washington, DC; Kevin Fisher, ASLA, Rhodeside & Harwell, Inc., Alexandria, Virginia; Thomas S. James, ASLA, Bohler Engineering, Sterling, Virginia; Edward M. Johnson, ASLA, Edward M. Johnson & Associates, Washington, DC; and Jess Zimbabwe, ASLA, Urban Land Institute's Daniel Rose Center for Public Leadership in Land Use, Washington, DC

The topic of discussion for the panel was the perception of the landscape architect; perceptions of those with whom we work regularly such as engineers, architects, and clients, as well as perceptions of our profession by the public and those we hold of ourselves. In these challenging economic and environmental times, are landscape architects being used to our fullest potential?

Tom James' experience at Bohler Engineering is that landscape architects are appreciated and that we have a niche in the realm of engineering. Many engineers find the profession a breath of fresh air and generally colleagues are receptive to new ideas. The strength of our profession is bringing the disciplines of engineering or architecture together with landscape architecture to form a more comprehensive approach to the design problem.

Kevin Fisher of Rhodeside & Harwell, a landscape architecture and planning firm, felt that outside consultants didn't always know what landscape architects could contribute. As much as it can, his firm tries to be involved with a project early on so it can have some influence on its role and how the space will evolve through the process. "Especially as more civil engineers have become knowledgeable about sustainable design in their own practices, they appreciate the knowledge that we bring to these elements; not just dressing up their work but actually integrating design into a project's engineering aspects. What we do has become more integrated into a project as people have become more aware of what landscape architects do."

There needs to be more engagement by landscape architects civically, sitting on planning boards, speaking up at those kinds of meetings, and also showcasing the diverse work that landscape architects can do.—Jess Zimbabwe

Lisa Delplace was asked if she is seeing a trend that has clients coming to them for more than just "place-making" and more for environmental mitigation. Are landscape architects seen more now as having the tools to cure the ills affecting the environment?

She replied that she has been in the profession long enough to not see this current surge of sustainability as something new. "When I went to school, there was also a sustainable movement, so my education was firmly grounded in using our natural resources wisely. But the new trend that I see is that our colleagues in architecture and engineering are joining us in that." There is a hundred-year history of landscape architects as environmental mitigators as seen through the likes of Olmsted and Jensen. Landscape architects do have a presence; it is not new but now we can guide the entire team in a direction that is sustainable.

Jess Zimbabwe has done a lot of public sector work including her previous position as director of the Mayor's Institute on City Design. She stated that her work is focused on educating those public sector leaders on how to be better clients. There are cities that "get it" and those cities are growing in the ranks. She feels there is "a fundamental misconception among public sector agencies about what landscape architects do or can do. It may be that a city's planning or parks director gets it, but decisions are made above that person by lay leaders, or city managers," who are the people with whom she works. Jess is not a landscape architect but is a member of ASLA because she believes in its mission. She believes that we are on the right track but that there **needs to be more engagement by landscape architects civically, sitting on planning boards, speaking up at those kinds of meetings, and also showcasing the diverse work that landscape architects can do**—so that we can start to counteract the simplified view that 'landscape architects do parks and parks alone—or gardens.'"

Roger Courtenay was asked if landscape architects should be prime consultants on more projects to increase the prominence of the profession.

To the general question of whether landscape architects should be priming more projects, Roger thinks we should be "more sensitive to the question of politics versus skill expectations" in situations such as the Eisenhower Memorial. He suggests restating the question: "Should we be concerned about what we're doing, rather than whether we are prime or not, and whether the role we have is still significant and appropriate? From the perspective of my own career, that has been very successful and I've had a meaningful role on many projects because of being able to, or having had the opportunity to find over the years those architects and professionals who respect what I contribute and with whom I have a collaborative design experience.

"We are a materialist, consumer-driven, object-oriented society. Place-making is more complicated: it's not object-oriented and is just not going to be as accessible to the general society. . . . History tells us that architects, being object-oriented, have been able to transcend this more easily . . . than maybe we as landscape architects have historically been able to. Some examples are Lawrence Halprin and Charles Eliot, first-class professionals who have taken us in the other direction.

"I think there's a middle ground between those two perspectives and that might be in the place where we at EDAW see a huge increase globally in our work in urban design in the public realm where we are leading projects. . . . **I don't think there's any doubt that we have the skills to lead, and that in the right milieu and environment we find that entrée and the people who are looking for that type of leadership.** So the key is finding the jobs that are suited to us. Urban regeneration is one of those areas finding landscape architects because of the specific skills we bring.

"To come back to the Eisenhower Memorial, I think that the short list of four designers . . . was based on some expectations about place-making there that would be . . . significantly architectural, just because of the overwhelming weakness of the architectural environment there.... Inside that I can tell you a little bit about our role: Joe Brown and I participated strongly in the interview with Frank Gehry and Craig Webb. There's an emerging collaborative idea there . . . we're the project managers as well as the landscape architects so we'll have a very, very strong role in facilitating, coordinating, and making sure that the thing's a success. We found our role—it's not a prime but will be significant."

Turning to Tom James, the moderator talked about the fame that winners of memorial competitions are likely to receive even to the point of becoming superstars. He asked Tom, if, in the end, these aren't really memorial landscapes? Why are the competitions falling in the realm of the architect—the World Trade Center, the Pentagon Memorial?

"Our strength and design approach is collaborative. The ideal blend is to have the architect, landscape architect, and civil engineer be involved in the initial development of the parti. As far as 'superstar'—I'm never comfortable with that. The bottom line is that we're serving humanity, and that fact should be first and foremost beyond any strict architectural bias or any preconceived notion. That is what drives my own passion and calling as a landscape architect, and I think that infiltrates every aspect of our profession."

The moderator asked Jess Zimbabwe to return to Roger's comments about the public realm: "Do you think the general public realizes how planned and designed the built environment is? Does it matter whether they recognize that?"

"I don't think it's particularly planned and designed. You can't really blame them because there are some noticeable examples of really badly planned and coordinated urban environments that they have to deal with every day. I think it would improve the professions, discourse, and environment eventually to have the public better informed.

"I think landscape architects as a profession should lay more claim to the term *urban design*. . . . Almost all landscape architects—especially those working in an urban context—are doing urban design by default."

Kevin Fisher was asked how we could make our work more prominent in the urban design field. Does our work really need to stand out and shock people so they realize it is something that has been thought about and designed?

I don't think there's any doubt that we have the skills to lead, and that in the right milieu and environment we find that entrée and the people who are looking for that type of leadership. So the key is finding the jobs that are suited to us.
—Roger Courtenay

Kevin felt it didn't "need to. . . . It could be something that people don't really notice but still enjoy and experience without being aware that it was planned or designed. For most landscape architects, I don't think that the reason that they are doing what they do is to be necessarily noticed by the general public. To be recognized by our peers certainly, but we're not out there putting banners up about our work—it's really about people enjoying, using and benefiting from the space."

The moderator then asked Edward Johnson, how we, as designers, can affect the way people live?

Mr. Johnson felt that so many people really don't have a clue about what architects or landscape architects do other than to draw. Most important is the need to educate our leadership not only locally but nationally. **"We need to have architects and landscape architects as senators and members of Congress—and also urban planners.** We need to begin to lobby our leadership across this land about the necessity of utilizing and implementing recommendations that we make into law. We are charged with the responsibility—those of us who work with the built environment and the natural environment."

"If we're going to influence how people think and to stimulate them to recognize the enormous contribution that landscape architects, architects, or urban planners make to civilization—then the media is where it needs to occur. . . . If we begin to take advantage of positions in educational institutions, government institutions, and private industry to impact publications and media people, we will go a long way quickly."

The moderator asked Lisa Delplace to discuss the role of ASLA. What do we need to be doing to make the work of landscape architects more prominent?

"Maybe we need to challenge ourselves as a modest profession to really speak out—particularly in cities where oftentimes people don't understand the kind of space they have and how it can be made better.

"I have been working in Chicago for several years now—a perfect example because when the mayor took a particular interest in changing the perception of Chicago, he began at the city core. If you look at Chicago now it's literally green at the core moving out to the suburbs. It's just the opposite of what you usually see. It's becoming a real revolution because the people demand it. Now they have experienced what it's like to be in a lush city and they want that.—Lisa Delplace

"I think we need—as landscape architects—to really work at the urban and civic level to say that people demand and need an appropriate space—a space that is not only interesting to be in but dynamic, that responds to the site it's on. We are place making for the people who inhabit those spaces."

The moderator then asked Lisa Delplace, "Two jurisdictions in the country do not require licensure for landscape architecture—Vermont and Washington, DC . . . how could the city not require licensure?"

Lisa replied that in the District, many of the laws on the books are arcane. "If a landscape architect were to provide services as a landscape architect, we would have to pass on tax to our clients because under the current classification we are considered 'landscapers.' ASLA has made a real push supporting many jurisdictions to have a practice act."

Edward Johnson, who is an architect, interjected that Washington is a unique, small city with large amounts of green space downtown so there has never really been a need to push for licensure of landscape architects. "It has been an extension of what architects do because until recently we have not had major challenging projects where there needs to be a serious focus on licensing landscape architects."

He also saw a tremendous need for the profession to focus more on construction estimating because we are impacting the natural environment in many ways. . . . In a recent project, he convinced a developer to rethink paving much of the site with asphalt to achieve LEED credits. . . . **Don't give up when the clients say no. Go back; re-think the way you are proposing it.** This approach is beneficial to us now and to those youngsters coming into the fields who will be our leaders."

Session Five: The Principles of the Principals

Moderator: Ryan Keith

Participants: Elisabeth Lardner, ASLA, Lardner/Klein Landscape Architects, PC; Faroll Hamer, ASLA, Department of Planning and Zoning, City of Alexandria, Virginia; Steven E. Lefton, ASLA, Urban Resource Group/Kimley-Horn & Associates, Herndon, Virginia; Jeff S. Lee, FASLA, Lee + Papa and Associates, Washington, DC; Robert W. Good, FASLA, Stephenson + Good; and Mark C. Gionet, ASLA, Lewis Scully Gionet, Inc, Vienna, Virginia

The panelists represented a cross section of established industry professionals in both the public and private realm. The event covered topics including landscape architecture history, critique and the current recession and its effects on the industry.

On the Topic of Starting a Landscape Architecture Firm

Elisabeth Lardner: "As a working mom for many years this gave me a lot of flexibility than if I'd been in a big firm. . . . Also being able to stay on the boards and having a lot of one-to-one contact were part of the advantages of having your own firm, . . . We began with a lot of public work which both kept us going and turned out to be what we really love doing. The ability to do the type of work you love to do is a prime advantage."

On the Topic of Multidisciplinary Firms

Steven Lefton: "Virtually everything I do is collaborative; it's the nature of our profession. But what drew me to the firm—and I've been there in two states for going on thirteen years—was the ability to have control . . . to be in the driver's seat, to be the point person leading a multidisciplinary team rather than playing a bit role, which is what I was seeing in some of the other firms that were working with ours, seeing that we could do this better and that as landscape architects we have the skill set to lead the project, to lead engineers, architects, and to drive the process."

Cities used to be considered unhealthy and the suburbs were healthy. Well that's completely flipped. Now the cities are healthy and the suburbs are where fat people drive a lot. That's where the couch potatoes live. —Faroll Hamer

On the Topic of Inspirational Landscape Designers

Faroll Hammer: "Laurie Olin and Tom Balsley because they do urban realm, which is what I've always been most interested in. . . . There's a huge back-to-the-city movement; it's not just empty nesters, it's young people. People are beginning to raise their families in cities now. Cities used to be considered unhealthy and the suburbs were healthy. Well that's completely flipped. Now the cities are healthy and the suburbs are where fat people drive a lot. That's where the couch potatoes live. So we've gone through a whole paradigm shift, a complete turnaround, and it's a huge opportunity for landscape architects. . . . Huge swaths of DC have gone through this; Arlington and Alexandria are going through it. . . . I'm thinking of Laurie Olin because I'm thinking of Bryant Park [in New York City], which we often talk about in Alexandria as a great urban space. Also Tom Balsley, a lesser-known landscape architect who also practices in New York City and does fantastic pocket parks. If you've never seen his work you should look it up; it's really superb."

On the Topic of the Future of Landscape Architecture

Steven Lefton: "If we put a marker at 1969 and fast forward one hundred years, when we look back I think we'll reflect on organizational rather than individual impact. Now the lines are much more blurred. When it was 'Olmsted' it was Olmsted. Today there is more collaboration, less pride of individual authorship and more focus on the team—more of a focus on the body of work produced by groups of people or organizations and less on that of the individual."

On the Topic of Landscape Architects as Self-promoters

Mark Gionet: "Historically, there have also been self-promoters. I don't think Olmsted and Olmsted's brothers lack that. Reading *The Devil in the White City* (by Erik Larson) points out that a strong personality is always a huge advantage in business and the business aspects of getting the work. . . . I think to myself 'Who is the person who put a man on the moon?' That was a team at NASA. But people do remember designers as a sole, crafty profession that has gotten this individual name associated with something—and I don't think that's necessarily going to change, in part because it's a way of making your mark on the artistic end of it."

On the Topic of Receiving Credit for Your Work

Bob Good: "I've never worried about that. I couldn't care less if my name is on the firm, to be honest. . . . But creativity tends to foster individualism just because of what it is and how it works. Putting together a team that can harness that creativity is even better."

Elisabeth Lardner: "For the past fifteen years, we've been so attracted to the shiny bauble, what photographs well and not what works for the community. I work on public works projects, they are grant-funded projects; they're not sexy, they're not glamorous, but they belong to the community. . . . I feel successful if the members of the community at the end of the day feel that they own the project."

On the Topic of Critique and Scrutiny within the Industry

Jeff Lee: "I was at the Dumbarton Oaks to hear Beth (Elizabeth) Meyer speak about her book *Sustaining Beauty*. Her premise is that it's not enough to say that a whole project is sustainable; you have to explain it in a creative way. She's challenging the profession, upping the ante and I find that inspirational. She's able to show examples of projects, some good, some bad, some excellent, some terrible, without actually leveling a judgment in terms of aesthetic quality or its worthiness in terms of what it's trying to achieve."

Farroll Hamer: "In addition to our not doing enough critiques or having enough dialogue within the profession, especially about plans or larger scale architecture projects, we don't do a good enough job communicating our ideas."

Steven Lefton: "It doesn't do a lot of good for us to sit around here and tell us whether we like each other's work; that doesn't really matter. . . . It's all about what the nonprofessional thinks. We need to ask, 'Is the user happy?' We need to figure out a way to better understand whether our constituents, the users and our clients, [are] pleased with our work."

Bob Good: "Someone once told me that design is all about knowing your parameters, and the more tightly defined they get, the better your design will be in response to them. Theoretically, if all you have to work with is mud and straw, then a critique says, 'Well that's nothing but mud and straw so it isn't worth very much.' But maybe that mud and straw creation was right on target for the boundaries that it was created within."

On the Topic of the Current Recession

Mark Gionet: "At some level we're a discretionary purchase for our clients, whether on the public or private side of the business. We're not a big profession, so proportionally we take a bigger hit. We're not an absolute necessity. You can shave off a little and things will still get done without us. The upside is that it will come back. The first thing that people want after they've been down in the dirt for a while is art, beauty, joy and recreation and your commercial clients need to sell things, and need that edge that landscape architecture provides."

Jeff Lee: "We need to call out the civil engineers as having a monopoly on fifty-year old details that exist in one blue book—and no one wants to change those details. I have many friends who are civil engineers, but they agree. They have all the canned details locked in, and the guys that give permits have the same details in their book, so every time we try to discuss innovative storm water systems where we can actually take a building and get rid of all the pipes—and save a client millions of dollars—try to get a civil engineer to work with you on that! . . . It's the civil engineers who fight us tooth and nail. And why? Because we have the solutions that may make their engineering technology obsolete."

Elisabeth Lardner: "Every time we have a recession we lose a generation in the profession. You can almost look at the hierarchy in the office and see the gap, which tells you when the last recession was. In the 1980s I worked as a daycare worker and waitress, but I stayed in the profession. Most people did not. How do we encourage the people coming out of school to stay in the profession during this recession, recognizing there's no good way to pay them?"

Steven Lefton: "A recession is a terrible thing to waste! If you wait until things get better, you've wasted an incredible opportunity to innovate and incubate for change, rather than waiting until civil engineers do better. We've got this capacity that three years ago we didn't have, because everyone was too busy

A strong personality is always a huge advantage in business and the business aspects of getting the work.—Mark Gionet

needing simply to meet their deadlines. There's time now in the system to change the code, to change the antiquated details, so we should just go do it; otherwise it will just be more of the same."

On the Topic of How To Weather the Current Recession

Mark Gionet: "What's interesting about the current recession is what game changers will come out of this. In the 1990s we went into [the recession] with people drawing by hand and came out of it a couple years later using computer-assisted drawing technology. School's a great place to wait out a downturn."

Elisabeth Lardner: "It's really hard to take a job outside the field, to take the chip off your shoulder and retain your self-confidence. So how do you keep your confidence up? You have to find your passion and you have to start working on that some more. . . . I had to learn how to draft, so I went to community college, took an irrigation class because on the West Coast at that time you couldn't get a job if you didn't know how to size pipe, and took a painting class. Travel if you don't have a mortgage and a family. See part of the world. Pay your way by working in a restaurant or bar; expand those horizons and see what kind of work is being done."

Jeff Lee: "Volunteer at something similar to neighborhood design services, provide pro bono services, work with the community. I think there are a lot of different ways that you can stay in the profession. It requires some tenacity."

Faroll Hamer: "You're not always going to be in front of a community with wonderful new ideas; sometimes they're very angry at your ideas, or with the developer's ideas, so any kind of facilitation skills you have, ways to calm people down, listening skills, or any kind of community group experience will be extremely useful if you decide to come back to landscape architecture."

On the Topic of Design after the Recession

Jeff Lee: "The hopeful part of what's happening in the field is that as the profession becomes more mainstream—and our fees and salary scale reflect that— we have the luxury of doing more research and development at the front end of a project. Not only does that put meat on our designs, but it drives the possible solutions."

FOUR MILE RUN RESTORATION MASTER PLAN

A 14-month planning effort was completed that involved inter-jurisdictional coordination between Arlington County and the City of Alexandria. In the joint project, the two jurisdictions initiated a master plan to transform the 2.3-mile stretch of the Four Mile Run study area from a utility "catch-all" to an environmentally focused community asset. As the prime planning and design consultant, Rhodeside & Harwell led a team of engineers, ecologists, hydrologists, and designers in the development of a master plan for this area.

The planning process included extensive community involvement through stakeholder round-table discussions, civic association presentations, a community-wide Visioning Event, and public Open Houses. The master plan was unanimously approved by City Council and the County Board of Supervisors in 2006. The implementation phase began 2007 with the firm's development of design guidelines. The City and County have embarked on the first phase of design: rehabilitation of the wetlands and near-stream areas.

RHODESIDE & HARWELL

LEGEND

- LOW FLOW CHANNEL, TRIBUTARIES AND DAYLIT STREAMS
- TREES AND FOREST
- EMERGENT WETLAND
- RIPARIAN EDGE PLANTING
- FLOODPLAIN PLANTING
- BANK STABILIZATION PLANTING
- GREEN OPEN SPACE
- MEADOW
- PEDESTRIAN AND CYCLIST BRIDGES, RAISED WALKWAYS OR RAMPS
- TRAILS
- INFORMAL STREAM CROSSINGS
- GRADE CONTROL STRUCTURE
- URBAN REDEVELOPMENT OPPORTUNITIES
- URBAN PLAZA OR URBAN OPEN SPACE

1. REORIENTED BALLFIELD
2. EXISTING BALLFIELD
3. RELOCATED BALLFIELD
4. REORIENTED MULTIPURPOSE FIELD
5. PROPOSED MULTIPURPOSE FIELD
6. INFORMAL 'PICK-UP' GAME AREA
7. PROPOSED BASKETBALL COURT
8. PROPOSED TENNIS COURT
9. PROPOSED COMMUNITY GARDENS
10. PROPOSED ALEXANDRIA & ARLINGTON NATURE CENTER
11. RELOCATED PARKING LOT
12. PROPOSED STREET WITH ADDITIONAL STREET PARKING
13. RECONNECTED TRIBUTARY
14. PROPOSED RECYCLING CENTER
15. WATER POLLUTION CONTROL PLANT DEMONSTRATION WETLAND
16. BOULDERING RECREATION AREA/ INFORMAL PLAY AREA
17. TRAILHEAD
18. EXISTING WOODROW WILSON BRIDGE MITIGATION WETLAND PROJECT
19. EXISTING SUBSTATION
20. GREENING OF WATER POLLUTION CONTROL PLANT (WPCP) TO INCLUDE GREEN ROOFS, GROUND SURFACE AND BUFFER TREATMENTS
21. EXISTING BASKETBALL PRACTICE COURT
22. MT VERNON AVENUE URBAN OPEN SPACE (WITH EVENT BOX & REST-ROOMS)
23. WATER PLAY AREA
24. URBAN OPEN SPACE ON RETAINED BRIDGE (WITH EXPERIENCE TOWER, CUTOUTS THROUGH BRIDGE, OVERHANGING PLATFORMS, CAFE & CANOE RENTALS)
25. RAMP WITH ADJACENT STORMWATER CASCADE
26. BIORETENTION AREA
27. PERFORMANCE PONTOON

BRIDGES

A. GEORGE WASHINGTON MEMORIAL PARKWAY
B. METRO
C. CSX RAIL
D. POTOMAC AVE (ROAD CURRENTLY UNDER CONSTRUCTION)
E. REUTILIZATION OF DISUSED BRIDGE AS GREEN OPEN SPACE WITH EXPERIENCE TOWER AND STORMWATER PLANTERS
F. REMOVAL OF DISUSED BRIDGE
G. EXISTING PEDESTRIAN/CYCLIST BRIDGE
H. ROUTE 1
I. MT VERNON AVE
J. PROPOSED WEST GLEBE ROAD VEHICULAR BRIDGE REALIGNMENT
K. REMOVAL OF EXISTING WEST GLEBE ROAD VEHICULAR BRIDGE
L. I395

RHODESIDE&HARWELL

NATIONAL AQUARIUM IN BALTIMORE

Rhodeside & Harwell worked closely with the National Aquarium to transform Pier 3 into a waterfront park that expresses the Aquarium's mission of environmental education and stewardship and provides a seamless visitor experience. The new waterfront park features paving, lighting, furnishings, planting and exterior exhibits that demonstrate the importance of protecting Maryland's native ecosystem and serve as a model of sustainable design.

Planting areas improve the microclimate on the pier and exhibit native plant communities from the coastal, piedmont, and mountain regions of Maryland. Below the plaza, a network of root paths lined with amended soil, aeration tubing, drain and irrigation lines interconnect the tree and other planting areas and improve growing conditions. Roof runoff is harvested for irrigation and surface runoff from the plaza is filtered through planting, soil, and aggregate layers. Custom unit pavers incorporate locally quarried aggregate and post-consumer waste materials.

A 37' x 20' granite map delineates the Chesapeake Bay watershed, with the outline of the bay, its tributaries and the Atlantic coastline from New York to North Carolina. Rhodeside & Harwell created the digital artwork used to cut and etch the map and worked closely with the granite fabricator to achieve the precise and elegant results.

RHODESIDE & HARWELL

US NATIONAL ARBORETUM

The US National Arboretum has a rich history, pre-dating its establishment by Congress in 1927. Much of this history is woven into the present-day Arboretum fabric. Rhodeside & Harwell has created landscape works at the site since 1998 and recently updated the Arboretum's Master Plan, including design of a new complex of gardens donated by the Chinese government. The Master Plan Update integrates sustainable design throughout the site's 446 acres, with a storm water management system of lakes, swales, and pools, new pathways, decks through sensitive forested areas and a rehabilitation of the fifty-year-old Asian Collections. We have renovated the Herb Garden and related grounds, while respecting the work of generations of landscape architects who preceded us, and with whom we continue to collaborate. Our design for the courts of the Bonsai and Penjing Museum displays this rare collection—the oldest in America—in an intimate and serene, sustainably designed contemplative space.

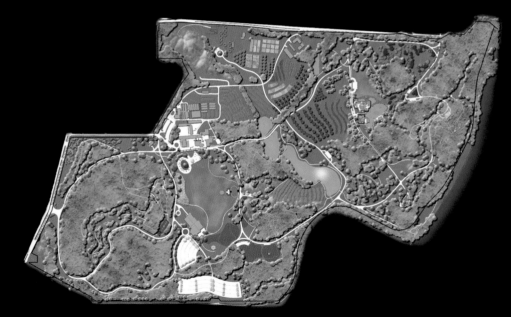

RHODESIDE&HARWELL

Landover Gateway Sector Plan

Port Towns Sector Plan

Capital Gallery

Steamtown National Historic Site

HITT Construction Headquarters

Alexandria Central

Dulles Corridor Metrorail

George Mason National Memorial

Bailey's Crossroads Planning Study

Branch Brook Park

National Zoological Park Kids Farm Exhibit

Amtrak Land Use Analysis

Norfolk Consolidated Courts Complex

DC Convention Center Interim Use

New Shade Structure w/Thatched Roof & Low Planted Screening

Fenced Consular Garden   Seating & Urn

US Embassy Africa

On Friday November 6, 2009, students in landscape design and landscape architecture from Virginia Tech (VT–Alexandria, Virginia) and The George Washington University (GW) gathered at GW's Alexandria Graduate Education Center for a discussion about their experience as students and their aspirations as future practitioners. The following is an abridged version of the lively discussion.

Moderators: Lisa Siri, ASLA, and Beth Carton, ASLA

Participants: Nick Colombo, Virginia Tech, second-year MLA; Sandra Nam, Virginia Tech, second-year MLA; Christina del Valle, GW, Graduate Certificate, Fall 2009; Allison Thurmond, Virginia Tech, working on thesis; Evelyn Nolan, GW, Graduate Certificate, Spring 2009; and Cristina Lewandowski, Virginia Tech, third-year MLA

Edited by: Ron M Kagawa, ASLA LEED AP

Moderator: "What influenced your decision(s) to enter landscape architecture?"

Sandra: "I had been working in New York City in various marketing positions. I like how landscape architecture engages a variety of other fields, for example ecology, urban planning and natural resources."

Evelyn: "I am originally from Chicago, with an undergrad specialization in Computer Science. . . . A few years ago I had an "aha!" moment when I was reading an article showing the work of some landscape architects, and I thought, 'That is beautiful; I would love to do that,' . . . and I found GW's program."

Cristina L.: "I also had a background in computers. I've been working in that area for many years, then realized that my life was not really a designed life, but one that was just happening. My 'aha!' moment came when I realized that there are people who design life, and I thought that I'd like to be part of that. That's how I came to GW's program."

How do you create new things by layering over existing things, rather than just tearing everything down?—Cristina L.

Nick: "There wasn't really a single 'aha!' moment for me. My undergrad degree was in urban history. I had interned with Baltimore City's Planning Department, and . . . with the National Park Service. In hindsight my choice of landscape architecture makes perfect sense. . . . I was working for an urban planning firm when I had the opportunity to work on design charrettes with landscape architects and to peer over their shoulders. Finally I asked them, 'What do you do when you're not here at community meetings?'"

Christina D.: "Rather than having an 'aha!' moment, my experience was more of an evolution. I had worked as a journalist for many years, a job with long hours and many frustrations. I wanted to combine my desire for public service . . . with something I loved to do."

Allison: "I grew up in western Oklahoma in a very rural area, on a ten-thousand-acre working cattle ranch. I began my undergraduate work at the University of Oklahoma in architecture, when I was too young to know what I was getting myself into. . . . I started doing research with one of the graduate professors in landscape architecture. Slowly I came to recognize that I'd rather be working in landscape architecture."

Moderator: "What are some of the landscapes that have influenced you? What do you envision yourself doing in landscape architecture?"

Cristina L.: "When I came to this country ten years ago, I realized that I knew the roads and names of buildings but not the names of trees! And that knowledge is what ties me to Romania, my native country. Gradually my interests developed into thinking about other questions: . . . How do you put together architecture and landscape? And how do you encourage people to live outside? Right now I'm interested in the old versus the new in architecture and landscape architecture. How do you create new things by layering over existing things, rather than just tearing everything down?"

Sandra: "The first designed landscape I grasped onto was my first house as a child, the first house we moved into. My parents were immigrants from Korea, and when they were able to buy a house they designed a Japanese garden around it. . . . By helping my parents with our Japanese garden I realized that you could manipulate land. But it wasn't until many years later that I realized that there could be a profession related to this."

Nick: "I grew up on Long Island: essentially 120 miles of parking lot! Not a great 'formative experience.' My interest in landscape architecture definitely came later, from the urban planning perspective. The neighborhood we lived in, in Baltimore, Rowland Park, was designed by Frederick Law Olmsted, Jr. It had such a different character than the urban grid of the rest of the city. . . . Even though Olmsted didn't design the houses themselves, by working with how the land is formed and oriented and how then the buildings fit into it, he made the neighborhood cohesive."

Moderator: "Is one of the strengths of your programs that you are being exposed across disciplines?"

Allison: "Landscape architecture is one of the few professions left where one is a generalist who manages specialized professions [and] can take a broader view, managing the views and goals of both clients and adjacent professions."

Sandra: "The strength of the programs is that we're being taught that we have to wear many hats when working in the field."

Nick: "As a laboratory for those studying landscape architecture, Washington, DC, is a fortunate place to be, because so much effort is spent on the landscape in comparison to almost any other city on earth, and one can see how things play out without having to go very far."

Moderator: "People used to say, 'landscape architects—they don't know their plants!' Are you learning enough about plant materials? . . . Are there other areas that would be useful to be improved?"

Evelyn: "We can always use more information, but not having everything covered in school also forces one to learn how to find more resources and to recognize that it's important to look for additional resources in *not having everything covered in school also forces one to learn how to find more resources and to recognize that it's important to look for additional resources.* —Evelyn

organizations and local institutions. . . . During my last semester at GW, I was thinking that I wasn't sure what I would do afterwards when I needed to further my knowledge. Then someone who'd taken part in the Master Gardener program at Hillwood Gardens in DC suggested I volunteer there, and that's what I'm doing now! I get to be out there as a gardener, . . . but it lets me witness what happens in the garden throughout the year. So, I think it should be up to us to use what we learned in the program, and take it from there."

Christina D.: "GW's program provides a huge emphasis on plant materials and horticulture, providing us a very good database of plants that will prosper in the DC area."

Nick: "I've taken plant classes at both GW and USDA and been impressed with how plants are taught locally. You always feel you should know more, but time limits you."

Evelyn: "We still have to deal with the issue that people don't understand what landscape architecture or design is. People think 'Oh the lawn, the trees!' But nobody thinks of making space. Plants are just one part of the palette of materials we have to work with."

Allison: "Within the palette of plants—at VT we don't focus enough on knowing the full extent of the plant palette's potential and limitations. . . . In the designs we work on we rarely are replicating the preferred environments of these plants."

Christina D.: "We're learning the right questions to ask—the right plant for the right place. I think that's the way to start in terms of learning a systematic way to identify the plants that can work within the local environment."

Evelyn: "Sustainability is a great way into explaining what we do as landscape architects. As people talk about green design and green technology, it's the perfect way to make what we do known, moving the conversation further along to discuss what landscape architecture is."

Cristina L.: "I think there is also simply a general ignorance of design, . . . an ignorance of having beautiful things around you in a designed environment."

Allison: "Another factor is that when landscape architects do their jobs well, people are unaware that the space was actually designed because the result seems so natural. **A job well done looks as though nothing was done!**"

Moderator: "Do you feel that your studies have prepared you for your professional career(s)?"

Sandra: "The beauty of the field we're entering is that we're always learning, and we always want to learn. What we are preparing ourselves for is working in an industry that is ever changing. **Now we're learning how to think—later we'll learn how to do.** I see the profession as a both craft and an art. As a craft, you have to be hands-on and do it. As an art, we need to understand we will need to develop a certain level of skill as we practice in the field."

Nick: "**There has been a value to having classmates who have not taken the same paths to the profession, offering all the students exposure to a range of perspectives and skills.** I learn as much from fellow students as I do from the faculty!"

Moderator: "Where do you see yourself in five years, or even fifteen years?"

Nick: "Employed!"

Allison: "Employed! I'm starting to look at firms, and find out where to get a job. It's tough—especially in this economy. We may all end up being fairly mobile to accommodate finding a job."

Evelyn: "I met with my financial planner when I started graduate school classes and he knew of an engineering program he thought I might want to enter, because he felt I could make a good living. But I said, "No! It's landscape design that interests me." For me, the struggle will be to leave the safety of my current career . . . how to transition to landscape architecture?"

Christina D.: "I have a dream: In fifteen years, I'd like to work with children to design sites important to them, for example, in inner city neighborhoods. . . . Children are the future, and if you can create beautiful spaces that children feel they have ownership of, it will let them feel they can create their world."

"I haven't yet developed the fifteen-second sound-byte answer to 'So, you're studying landscape architecture. What do you do?' . . . When I tried explaining it to my grandmother, she smiled and nodded after hearing it. Then she turned to her friend and introduced me saying I was going back to school to get an associates' degree in landscaping!"

—Nick Colombo

Sandra: "Whether five or fifteen years from now, I'm just hoping to be inspired every day by what I'm doing."

Moderator: "In the future, what would you like your peers to remember you for?"

Allison: "**I will be very satisfied if, by the end of my career, I've done work that is consistently thoughtful and had a direct impact making each site a distinctive place.** Consistently producing that type of work over decades will, I think, be harder to achieve than it sounds!"

Evelyn: "I'm thinking less about how my peers would be thinking about me than about the people who've spent time within my spaces and enjoyed them, even if they didn't know it was my work!"

Christina D.: "I really share that feeling."

Nick: "**If you love what you do, and put yourself into your work and continue to learn and get something out of your work, that's the ideal career.** And if you accomplish that well enough for it to also be evident to those with whom you work, then I think you've done pretty well!"

Sandra: "Have your peers regard you as a dependable person; that would be important because in this profession you need support and you want to know that you can go to your peers. . . . Also, I wish there could be more opportunities for this type of discussion, whether it's with our generation of students or with practitioners, but more conversations about the field."

Nick: "The only times we as a profession get together is at big conferences where there is a lot going on. But it would be very nice if we . . . could get together with people from other firms and schools within our lines of work to be able to compare notes. We could meet here in five, ten, and fifteen years—and each of us brings one student with us.

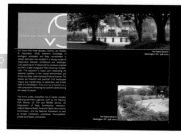

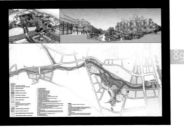

page
90

Top left: Alain Jaramillo
Bottom left: Elliot Rhodeside
Right: Steve Uzzell

page
9

Elli

page
92

Top left: Elliot Rhodeside
Top right: Ron Blunt
Bottom: Rhodeside & Harwell, Inc.

page
9

Stev

page
94

Top left: Rhodeside & Harwell, Inc.
Bottom left: Maxwell Mackenzie
Top center: Steve Uzzell
Bottom center: Ron Blunt
Top right: Rhodeside & Harwell, Inc.
Middle right: Steve Uzzell
Bottom right: Rhodeside & Harwell, Inc.

page
95

Top
Top
Top
Mid
Cent
Mid
Bott
Bott

Acknowledgments

Potomac Chapter Executive Committees

2009/2010
Bethany Carton, President-Elect
Lisa Siri, President
Karen Kumm Morris, Past President
Ron Kagawa, Trustee
Sarah Couchman, Secretary
Mark Mastalerz, Treasurer
Jeanette Ankoma-Sey, Member-at-Large
Adele Ashkar, Member-at-Large
Paul Kelsch, Member-at-Large

2008/2009
Lisa Siri, President-Elect
Karen Kumm Morris, President
Ron Kagawa, Past President
Faye Harwell, Trustee
Bethany Carton, Secretary
Mark Mastalerz, Treasurer
Jeanette Ankoma-Sey, Member-at-Large
Adele Ashkar, Member-at-Large
Melissa Rainer, Member-at-Large

2007/2008
Karen Kumm Morris, President-Elect
Ron Kagawa, President
Lisa Delplace, Past-President
Faye Harwell, Trustee
Marci Drury, Secretary
Lisa Siri, Treasurer
Jeanette Ankoma-Sey, Member-at-Large
Adele Ashkar, Member-at-Large
Melissa Rainer, Member-at-Large
Josh Serck, Member-at-Large
Chris Shaheen, Member-at-Large

2006/2007
Ron Kagawa, President-Elect
Lisa Delplace, President
Heather Modzelewski, Past President
Faye Harwell, Trustee
Amy Neiberline, Secretary
Ryan Keith, Treasurer
Jeanette Ankoma-sey, Member-at-Large
Barbara Deutsch, Member-at-Large
Robert Good, Member-at-Large

Potomac Chapter Roster
January 11, 2010

Lindsey Abbott, Associate
Mary Abe
Edward H. Able, Jr., Honorary
René Manuel Albacete
Joel D. Albizo, Affiliate
Richard J. Alexander
Robert D. Anderson
Jeanette A. Ankoma-Sey
Richard L. Arentz
Linda Ashby, Associate
Adele N. Ashkar
Craig Atkins
Bruce Babbitt, Honorary
Claudia Barragan, Affiliate
Irene Bartnik
Claire Bedat
Jill Bellenger
Richard Bensman
Kenneth A. Berg
Jason Berner, Associate
Charles E. Beveridge, Honorary
Randall J. Biallas, Honorary
Bartlett A. Bickel
Daniel P. Biggs
Charles Birnbaum, Fellow
Leonard Kurt Blakley
Earl Blumenauer, Honorary
Sarah S. Boasberg, Honorary
Ronald Bogle, Affiliate
Keli Bosack, Associate
Stephanie Bothwell
Ryan Bouma
Sharon E. Bradley
Sheila A. Brady, Fellow
J. Brooks Breeden, Fellow
Nancy J. Brown
Dale Bumpers, Honorary
Katie Burney

Susan Cahill-Aylward, Honorary
Gabriela Canamar
Robert E. Capper
Dennis B. Carmichael, Fellow
Russ Carnahan, Honorary
Bethany Carton
Bruno P. Carvalho
Jeffrey V. Catts
Clarence Chaffee, Honorary
Ching-Fang Chen
Jacalyn Chnowski, Associate
Zachary D. Christeson
Thomas E Clark
Matthew V. Clark
Marilyn Clemens
Kathryn S. Cochrane
Laurence E. Coffin, Jr., Fellow
Beatriz D. Coffin, Fellow
Darian A. Copiz
Susi Cora, Affiliate
Beata B. Corcoran
Brian E. Cornell
Sarah Couchman, Associate
Roger Guy Courtenay, Fellow
Drew Crowder, Affiliate
Ralph J. D'Amato, Jr.
Rhonda S. Dahlkemper
Geneva L Davenport, Associate
Marie Davis, Affiliate
Sarah H. Davis
Lisa E. Delplace
Sharon H. Dendy
Amol M. Deshpande
Barbara L. Deutsch
Alain C. deVergie, Fellow
Jimmy Dick
Todd M. Dickey
Dennis Dixon
James A. Dobbin
Paul Dolinsky
Martha Donnelly

Sara M. Downing, Associate
Marci Drury
Aiman E. Duckworth
Aladino Duke
Amanda J. Eberly
Jeron O. Eberwein
Carla Ellern
Ann E. English
Chester L. Eva
Matthew Evans, Fellow
Florence Everts
Yunhui Connie Fan
Edward A. Feiner, Honorary
Stacilyn Feldman, LEED AP
Aaron Feldman-Grosse
Lila Fendrick
John Craig Fennell
Liesel W. Fenner
Darwin J. Feuerstein
Ron Figura, Affiliate
Sara Fiore, Associate
Kevin Fisher
Jonathan Fitch
Roger A. Foley, Affiliate
Melanie A. Fosnaught
Michael Furbish, Affiliate
Susanne Fyffe
Stephen G. Gang
Allan D. Garnaas
Brad C. Garner
John J. Gattuso
John L. Gavarkavich
Mark C. Gionet
Deon Glaser
Parris Glendening, Honorary
Aaron R. Goetz, Associate
Sarah Elaine Goodenow
Peter Gorman, Affiliate
Bernard Grace
Wilton Griffiths
Eric D. Groft

Elizabeth Guthrie
Linda Hales, Affiliate
Lucia Bowes Hall
Faroll Hamer
Edward G. Hamm
Mary L. Hanson, Honorary
Hillary Hanzel, Associate
Brandon Hartz
Faye B. Harwell, Fellow
Douglas A. Hays
Jennifer R. Hefferan
Joseph W. Heilman, Associate
Loren Helgason
Christina Hicks, Associate
Christine Hoeffner
Mark A. Holsteen
Joan P. Honeyman
Vance R. Hood, Honorary
Don Hoover
Donovan E. Hower, Fellow
William Hudnut, Honorary
Nancy L. Hughes
William Hutchings
Joseph Imamura, Associate
Nathan Imm
Brian Jacobson
Thomas S. James
Sareena Jerath, Affiliate
Edward M. Johnson
Elizabeth K. Johnson
Catherine E. Jones, Associate
Paxton Holt Jordan
Maureen DeLay Joseph
Daniel Jost
David W. Judd, Jr.
Ron M. Kagawa
Brian P. Kane
John F Kane, Affiliate
Eugene A. Keller
Craig Kelly
Paul Kelsch

Paul F. Killmer, Associate
Peter Kirsch, Honorary
Robert A. Kish
Norbert Kraich, Honorary
Matthew Kwiatkowski
Mary Landrieu, Honorary
Mark X. LaPierre
Elisabeth Lardner
Robert LaRoche
Marsha A. Lea
Kathy LeDain, Affiliate
Paul E. Lederer
Celia Sau W. Lee, Associate
Jeff S. Lee, Fellow
Steven E. Lefton
Ronald C. Leighton, Honorary
John Lightle, Associate
Peter H. Liu
Judy Lo
Stacy Loggins, Associate
Robin Lollar, Associate
Gregory Long, Associate
Cheryl K. Lough
Corinne Lynch, Associate
Tim Madden, Associate
Meg Maguire, Honorary
Mary Marcinko, Associate
Bonnie B. Markle
James Masciuch, Associate
Mark J. Mastalerz
Michael D. Mastrota
John H. McCarty
Craig A. McClure
Adrienne McCray
John D. McEachern
Christine McEntee, Affiliate
Robert M. McGinnis
Ed McMahon, Honorary
Patricia A. McManus
Rodney P. Mercer
Paul Meyers

Curtis A. Millay
Zandra Miller, Honorary
Iris Miller
Elizabeth Miller
Amy M. Mills
Heather Hammatt Modzelewski
Ryan Moody, Associate
Karen Kumm Morris
Robert H. Mortensen, Fellow
Sarah R. Moulton, Associate
Christopher Munson
Callum I. Murray
Milford D. Myers
Darwina L. Neal, Fellow
Nicholas Nelson
Bill Neus, Affiliate
David T. Norden
Mark Alan Novak
Hilary Oat-Judge, Associate
Molly A. Oliver, Associate
David A. Omidy, Associate
Mark Oxley, Affiliate
Daniel Park
John G. Parsons, Fellow
James T. Penrod
R. Max Peterson, Honorary
Keith Pitchford, Affiliate
Richard J. Pittman
William R. Pittman, Jr.
Donna Pivik
Joseph Plumpe
Theresa Polizzi
Deana Poss
Colin Powell, Honorary
William J. Prunka, Affiliate
Jane L. Przygocki
Phillip L. Puzick
Dan Quellette, Affiliate
Carrie Rainey, Associate
William K. Reilly, Honorary
Karie Reinertson, Affiliate

Elliot I. Rhodeside, Fellow
Brian Richards
Chad Michael Rinker
Jim Roberts, Affiliate
Trini M. Rodriguez
Pat S. Rosend
Chase Rynd
Brandon Sackett
Albert Salas
Harrison G. Saunders
Marisa N. Scalera
Richard Schubach, Affiliate
Allyson Schwartz, Honorary
Sunny Jung Scully, Fellow
John Sekerak, Jr.
Geoffrey Sharpe
Bang Shon
Cary Simmons, Associate
Sara E. Sinclair
Wannapa L. Siriamnuaypas
David Skalka, Affiliate
William C. Skelsey
Nancy Slade, Associate
Jeremy Smith
David R. Smith, Affiliate
William E. Smith, Jr., Affiliate
Glenn LaRue LaRue Smith
Robert E. Snieckus
Philip G. Snyder, Affiliate
Nancy C. Somerville, Honorary
Diane Sparks, Associate
Jeff B. Speck, Honorary
David H. Steigler
Adam J. Steiner
Brian J. Stephenson
Christopher M. Stevens
Sallie P. Stewart
William J. Stinger
Edward H. Stone II, Fellow
Kevin Joseph Tankersley
Matthew J. Tauscher

Stephen P. Tawes
Drew J. Taylor
Louise H. Taylor
J. William Thompson, Fellow
Floyd A. Thompson III
Robert B. Tilson, Fellow
Tanya Topolewski
Charles H. Trace, Jr.
Bing C. Tung
Clark P. Turner, Affiliate
Patricia Tyson, Affiliate
Meredith Upchurch
James van Sweden, Fellow
Michael Vergason, Fellow
Ellen L. Vogel
Kathy Von Bredow
Gary A. Wagner
Phyllis S. Wallenmeyer
Tim S. Walters, Associate
Charles R. Watkins
Elizabeth M. Wehrle
Bradley E. Wellington
Lauren Wheeler, Affiliate
J. Mark White
Annette Whitehurst
Nicole K. Whiteside
Robin Annette Wiatt
Theodore A. Willger
Guy Morgan Williams
Gary Douglas Wimberly
Amy Winter
Jessica G. Wolff
Lindy L. Wolner
Tina Woods-Smith
Darryl R. Wright
Amy Yu, Associate

Potomac Chapter Member Affiliations

Adtek Engineers, Inc.
AECOM—Alexandria
Allan Garnaas Associates
America's Promise Alliance
American Architectural Foundation
American Institute of Architects
American Society of Landscape Architects
American University
Americans for the Arts
Architect of the Capitol
Arentz Landscape Architects, LLC
Ault, Clark & Associates, Ltd.
Ayers/Saint/Gross Architects + Planners
B C Consultants
Beth Wehrle Landscape Architects
Bowman Consulting Group, Ltd.
Bradley Site Design, Inc.
Brian J. Stephenson & Company
Calvert County Department of Planning and Zoning
Carderock Stone/Tri-State Stone and Building Supply
The Care of Trees
Carvalho & Good, PLLC
Charles Luck Stone Center
Charles P. Johnson & Associates, Inc.
City of Alexandria, Recreation, Parks and Cultural Activities
City of Alexandria, Department of Planning
Clark Turner Companies
Clinton and Associates Landscape Architects
Coffin and Coffin Landscape Architects
Community Design & Development
Council of Landscape Architectural Registration Boards
DCA Landscape Architects, Inc.
Dewberry
District Department of Transportation
Dobbin International Inc.
E. M. Johnson and Associates
Edens & Avant
Elizabeth K. Johnson, Landscape Architect
Fairfax County Master Gardeners' Association, Inc
Fairfax County Park Authority
Florence Everts Associates
Furbish Company, LLC
Fyffe Landscape Architecture
G. Smith Studio, LLC

Garden Gate Landscaping, Inc.
Gardenwise, Inc.
Gensler
The George Washington University
Government Services IPT
Greenhorne & O'Mara, Inc.
Hanson & Molloy
Historic American Landscape Survey
HNTB Corporation
HOK, Inc.
Interlocking Concrete Pavement Institute
International Association of Fish and Wildlife Agencies
John Shorb Landscaping, Inc
Jordan Honeyman Landscape Architecture
The Kane Group LLC
LandDesign Inc
Landscape Architecture Bureau LLC
Landscape Architecture Foundation
Landscape Forms/Barbara Nolan, Inc.
LaPierre Studio
Lardner/Klein Landscape Architects
Las Vegas Sands Corporation
The Lessard Architectural Group
Lee + Papa and Associates
Lessard Architectural Group
Lewis Scully Gionet, Inc.
Lila Fendrick Landscape Architecture & Garden Design
Loiederman Soltesz Associates, Inc.
Mahan Rykiel Associates
Martha Donnelly & Associates
Maryland-National Capital Park and Planning Commission
McEachern and Associates
Michael Vergason Landscape Architects, Ltd.
Montgomery County Department of Environmental Protection
Moody Landscape Architecture
Mortensen Associates
National Building Museum
National Cemetery Administration
National Park Service
Natural Resources Design, Inc.
Niles Bolton Associates
NVblu, Inc.
OCULUS
Oehme, van Sweden & Associates, Inc.
Ohio State University
Outdoor Illumination, Inc.

Parker Rodriguez, Inc.
Parsons Management Consultants
PBS&J
Peter Liu Associates, Inc.
PHRA P.C.
Pitchford Associates, Ltd.
PM Garden Design
Prince William County Park Authority
Rhodeside & Harwell, Inc.
Rodgers Consulting
Roger Foley Photography
RTKL Associates, Inc.
Seraphic Land Design
SIRI, LLC
SmithGroup, Washington, DC
StressCrete Group
STUDIO39 Landscape Architecture, P.C.
3 Design Consulting, LLC
Tilson Landscape Company
Toole Design Group, LLC
Trace Inc.
True Turtle Real Estate
Turf Equipment and Supply Company
TWS Design, Inc.
United States Botanic Garden
Urban Engineering & Associates
Urban Land Institute
Urban Resource Group/Kimley-Horn & Associates, Inc.
Urban, Ltd.
US Department of State
US Department of the Interior
US General Services Administration, Center for Urban Development
US Green Building Council
US House of Representatives
US Senate
USDA Natural Resources Conservation Service
Victor Stanley, Inc.
Virginia Department of Transportation
Virginia Railway Express
Virginia Tech, Washington-Alexandria Center
Walter L. Phillips, Inc.
Walton Madden Cooper, Inc.
Washington Post Company

Potomac Chapter Honors

Note: Many of the Chapter's Fellows were inducted years before the Washington Chapter, later the Potomac Chapter, was formed. However, since they were Washington, DC members of National ASLA, and lived to become members of the local chapter after it was established, they are included here.

Fellows

Abbott, Stanley W.	1952
Andrews, Robert W.	1964
Ballard, Edward B.	1965
Birnbaum, Charles A.	1996
Brady, Sheila A.	2005
Brown, Joseph	1992
Carmichael, Dennis B.	1999
Carnes, William Gary	1953
Coffin, Beatriz de Winthuysen	1995
Coffin, Laurence E., Jr.	1981
Collins, Lester	1964
Courtenay, Roger	2007
De Silets, Eugene	1960
De Vergie, Alain C.	2005
Dodge, Carlton	1975
Draper, Earle Sumner	1927
Elliot, Charles W., II	1938
Evans, James Matthew	2003
Ewald, Walter	1957
Fay, Frederick A.	1957
Freeman, Raymond	1967
Gillette, Charles F.	1933
Good, Robert W.	2001
Greely, Miss Rose	1936
Griswold, Ralph	1933
Hanke, Byron R.	1974
Harris, Lynn M.	1965
Harwell, Faye B.	2008
Hays, Douglas A.	2010
Hopkins, Alden B.	1958
Hower, Donovan E.	1980
Kennedy, Sidney S.	1961
Kruse, Arthur	1924
LaGasse, Alfred B.	1974
Lasch, Mary Ann	1998
Lea, Marsha A.	2010
Lee, Jeff S.	2007
Mortenson, Robert H.	1980
Neal, Darwina L.	1982
Palmer, Meade	1958
Parker, Donald	1970
Parker, Gary	1965
Parsons, John	1984
Ramsdell, Charles H.	1916
Rhodeside, Elliot I.	2004
Sager, Merel S.	1952
Schulteis, Henry	1956
Scully, Sunny Jung	2000
Simonson, Wilbur	1940
Stone, Edward H., II	1974
Tilson, Robert B.	2005
Trotter, Morris E., Jr.	1958
Tuttle, Ronald W.	1995
van Sweden, James A.	1993
Vergason, Michael	2005
Vint, Thomas C.	1948
Walker, Hale	1957
Wells, William	1969
Wirth, Conrad L.	1948
Wright, David	1979
Zach, Leon	1938

Chapter Presidents

Kruse, Arthur	1946
Jeffers, Thomas C.	1948–1951
Abbott, Stanley W.	1952
Palmer, Meade	1954
Hendee, Myron	1960
Ballard, Edward	1960–1962
Freeman, Raymond	1963–1964
Dodge, Carlton	1965–1966
Bergman, Robert	1967
Bright, John	1969

Adele N. Ashkar, ASLA, is associate professor and Director of the Landscape Design Program at The George Washington University. She earned a BFA in landscape architecture at the Rhode Island School of Design and an MLA at the Harvard Graduate School of Design. She worked at the Office of Dan Kiley in Charlotte, Vermont, followed by stints at HOK in New York and Washington, DC. Adele was Potomac Chapter president in 2002–2003, and then sat on the Constitution and Bylaws and the Nominating Committees. She has been a member-at-large on the Executive Committee for several years.

Bethany A. Carton, ASLA, graduated from Iowa State University with a bachelor's in landscape architecture. She has worked for the Office of James Burnett in California and is currently a Park Planner for the City of Alexandria's Department of Recreation, Parks and Cultural Activities. She has been on the faculty of the Landscape Design Program at The George Washington University since 2008. She has been a guest lecturer at the University of Maryland and involved in student outreach for Iowa State University. She served on the Executive Committee as Chapter secretary in 2008–2009 and as president-elect in 2009–2010.

Ron M. Kagawa, ASLA, LEED AP, served as president of the Potomac Chapter in 2000–2001 and 2007–2008 and is 2009–2012 Chapter trustee. He holds an undergraduate degree in landscape architecture from the University of Texas–Arlington and a graduate degree in architecture from Virginia Tech—both with academic honors. As a landscape architect, he has served on the faculty of The George Washington University's Landscape Design Program in Washington, DC, since 1988. Ron is the Division Chief of Park Planning, Design and Capital Development with the City of Alexandria's Department of Recreation, Parks and Cultural Activities.